Wildlife Toys in Wood

Wildlife Toys in Wood

Lee Lindeman & Pat Harste

• • • • • • • • • •

 Sterling Publishing Co., Inc. New York

The authors would like to thank George Ross for the beautiful color and black-and-white photographs, Stephen Donelian for his expert assistance, Plaid Enterprises for supplying Folk Art Acrylic Color, and WesTrim Crafts for the beads.

Library of Congress Cataloging-in-Publication Data

Lindeman, Lee.
    Wildlife toys in wood / by Lee Lindeman and Pat Harste.
        p. cm.
    Includes index.
    ISBN 0-8069-8666-2
    1. Wooden toy making. 2. Animals in art. I. Harste, Patricia.
II. Title.
TT174.5.W6L55   1993
745.592—dc20   92-41345
                                                                CIP

9 8 7 6 5 4 3 2

Published by Sterling Publishing Company, Inc.
387 Park Avenue South, New York, N.Y. 10016
© 1993 by Lee Lindeman and Patricia Harste
Distributed in Canada by Sterling Publishing
% Canadian Manda Group, P.O. Box 920, Station U
Toronto, Ontario, Canada M8Z 5P9
Distributed in Great Britain and Europe by Cassell PLC
Villiers House, 41/47 Strand, London WC2N 5JE, England
Distributed in Australia by Capricorn Link Ltd.
P.O. Box 665, Lane Cove, NSW 2066
Manufactured in the United States of America
All rights reserved

Sterling ISBN 0-8069-8666-2

Contents

• • • • • • • • • • • •

Introduction 7
Before You Begin 7
Materials 7
Tools and Equipment 7
Safety Precautions 8
General Directions 9
Making the Patterns 9
Left and Right 9
Transferring Patterns and Marks 9
Stacking Wood 9
Bonding Wood 9
Cutting Wood 9
Whittling 10
Sanding 11
Drilling Holes 11
Gluing and Clamping 11
Countersinking Screws 12
Countersinking Brads 12
Cutting Beads in Half 12
Painting and Finishing 13

PROJECTS
North America
  1. Bullfrog 17
  2. Rattlesnakes 21
  3. Wood Duck Paddle Toys 26

4. Whale and Dolphin Mobile 30

5. American Alligator 35

6. Pond Slider Turtles 39

South America

7. Scarlet Macaw 42

8. Toucan 51

9. Spider Monkeys 58

Africa

10. Lion Pull Toy 64

11. Giraffe Pull Toy 70

12. Zebra Hobbyhorse 78

Asia

13. Goldfish Bowl 82

14. Greater Pandas 89

15. Tiger Hobbyhorse 94

16. Asian Elephant Pull Toy 98

Australia

17. Koalas 107

18. Tropical Fish Aquarium 111

19. Shark School Paddle Toy 118

20. Pink Cockatoo 121

Index 126

Metric Equivalents Table 127

[Color photos follow page 32]

Introduction

. . . .

Wildlife Toys in Wood is dedicated to all the magnificent animals inhabiting the earth. The animals that were selected as projects for this book are grouped by the five continents on which they are found. A brief biography containing important information and fascinating facts at the beginning of each project will help you better understand the animals that you will be creating.

Before You Begin

To save time, read through the project's directions both to familiarize yourself with them and enable you to gather the materials, tools, and equipment you will need. Refer to the "General Directions" for the various techniques used in making the projects.

Materials

The Materials list at the beginning of each project is always presented in the same order, making it an easy reference when gathering or shopping for materials. Lumber, dowelling, miscellaneous wood items such as beads and axle pegs, drill bits, brads, and screws are listed from the smallest size of the product to the largest. The paint colors are, with few exceptions, listed in the order in which they are used. The last item listed is the type of protective coating to be applied. Unless otherwise specified, use a water-base varnish in the type of finish recommended.

Lumber and dowelling estimates allow for waste plus a safety margin when handling them in a scroll saw. The dimension of the lumber specified in the Materials list is the nominal or pre-milled size and is also part of the name of the lumber. For example, $1/4 \times 5\frac{1}{4}$ clear pine lattice actually measures $7/32'' \times 5^{3}/_{16}''$.

Tools and Equipment

The following is a list of the tools and equipment needed to make all the projects. Some of the items are not required for every project, and any additional tools needed are listed in the project's Materials list.

Pencil for tracing patterns and marking measurements

Tracing paper for tracing or enlarging patterns

Graphite paper for transferring patterns onto wood (carbon paper can be substituted)

Dressmaker's carbon for transferring patterns onto fabric

Masking tape for securing patterns while they are being transferred

Cellophane tape for taping two-part patterns together

Double-sided masking tape for adhering stacked wood pieces together before sawing

Sharp scissors for cutting paper patterns, fabric pieces, and trims

Flexible ruler for accurate measuring of small areas (we recommend the Schaedler Precision Ruler, which is available in the commercial art department of art-supply stores)

18″ metal ruler for measuring flat items and as a guide when drawing straight lines

Pencil compass for drawing circles

Safety glasses for eye protection

Scroll saw for cutting wood and long lengths of dowelling

Coping saw for cutting short lengths of dowelling or where specified in a project

Whittling knife for rounding edges, making angles, and cutting beads in half

Wood vise for holding a piece securely when using a coping saw or drilling into the edge of a piece

Clamps for clamping wood pieces being bonded or glued, or for securing wood pieces to the work surface when sanding or when drilling into the face of a piece (use spring clamps, C-clamps, bar clamps, or handscrews)

Hand drill for drilling holes (an adjustable-speed power drill can also be used)

Drill bit and spade bits: see the project's Materials list for sizes

Drill stop for drilling accurate hole depths

½″ **countersink bit** for drilling a cone-shaped depression into a drilled pilot hole so that the head of an inserted and tightened screw will be below the surface of the wood

Small hammer for driving brads and cutting beads in half

Nail set for sinking brads below the surface of the wood and for making a depression in wood before using a hand drill

Screwdrivers for driving screws (use a screwdriver that matches the screw-head type)

Medium (150-grit), fine (220-grit), and super-fine (400-grit) sandpapers for sanding edges and surfaces smooth, and for sanding between coats of paint or finish

Tack cloth for wiping sawdust from wood pieces after they have been sanded (store the tack cloth in a screw-top jar to prevent it from drying out)

Wood glue for adhering raw wood to raw wood (for applications where clamping is not possible, we recommend using a cyanoacrylate glue, which bonds in seconds)

Waterproof wood glue: use as directed for tub toys

Tacky glue: use as specified in the directions for adhering fabric, trims, and painted wood to painted wood

Small dish for holding glue

Toothpicks for applying glue to small areas

½″ **flat brush** for applying glue to large areas

Paste wood filler for filling bead half-holes, gaps in construction, and covering countersunk nails and brads

No. 000, 5, and 7 round brushes for painting details

¼″, ½″, and 1″ **flat brushes** for painting small to large areas

Paint palette or ceramic dish for holding paint

Jar and water for washing brushes

Paper towelling for drying brushes

Safety Precautions

- These toys are intended for play by people ages 7 and up.
- Always wear safety glasses when sawing, drilling, whittling, or sanding.
- Always wear short sleeves and keep long hair tied back and out of the way when using power tools.
- Never wear rings, bracelets, or a watch when using power tools.
- To prevent interruptions when using power tools, it is best to take the phone off the hook and make sure small children and pets are safely out of the way.
- When using a scroll saw, make sure that the safety guard is down or in position before you begin to saw.
- Always turn a scroll saw off when it is not being used.
- Never turn off a scroll saw while the blade is still in the wood as the blade could break when power is restored.

General Directions

• • • • • • • • • • •

Making the Patterns

Most of the patterns in this book are actual size and ready to use. Secure tracing paper over the pattern, and use a pencil to trace the outline as well as painting lines, dashed positioning lines, positioning dots, and so on.

To enlarge a reduced pattern, you can either have the pattern enlarged at a photocopying shop (each box of the grid border equals 1″) or you can enlarge it by hand. To enlarge a pattern by hand, first draw lines across the pattern to connect the grid lines. Count the boxes across each edge to determine the size of tracing paper you will need. Rule the tracing paper into 1″ squares, making the same number of squares that are on the pattern. Then copy the pattern, line for line, onto the tracing paper.

To complete a half-pattern, trace the half-pattern shown in the book onto tracing paper. Turn the tracing over, align the dashed line on the tracing over the dashed line on the pattern in the book, and then trace the half-pattern again.

To complete a two-part pattern, trace both pattern halves onto separate sheets of tracing paper, align the dotted line on one half over the dotted line on the other half, and tape the two halves together.

Left and Right

Unless otherwise stated, left and right always refer to the animal's left and right sides. The left and right of all other items indicate your left and right as you view the items on the work surface.

Transferring Patterns and Marks

For maximum strength, position the patterns on the wood so that the longest dimension of the pattern is parallel with the grain of the wood.

To transfer a pattern onto wood, place graphite paper over the wood with the graphite side facing down. Use masking tape to secure it to the wood. Place the pattern on top and secure it with tape. Use a pencil to retrace all lines and positioning dots onto the wood; then remove the papers.

Cut out the piece on a scroll saw. Turn the pattern over to reverse the image, and transfer the painting lines, positioning dots, and so forth to the other side of the piece. Some projects (such as the Lion Pull Toy) don't have the same leg positions on both sides of the body, so be sure to read the project's directions before proceeding.

To transfer a pattern onto fabric, tape the fabric to the work surface. Place dressmaker's carbon (carbon side down) over the fabric and tape to secure. Place the pattern on top and tape it also. Use a pencil to retrace all lines.

Stacking Wood

For fast cutting of two identical pieces, use double-sided tape to adhere two lengths of lumber together. Be sure the grain of both lengths runs in the same direction. Transfer the pattern outline to the top of the stacked wood and cut the pieces out in a scroll saw. If the pieces must also be drilled for axle peg holes, mark the hole position and drill through the stack before separating the pieces.

Bonding Wood

To bond two pieces of wood together, run a continuous, thin bead of wood glue evenly across the face of each piece (see 1). Place the glued faces together with the edges aligned and clamp at each corner. Allow the bonded wood to set for at least four hours before transferring the pattern onto it and cutting it out.

Cutting Wood

If more than one pattern outline has been transferred onto a length of wood, cut between the outlines to make separate, more manageable pieces.

To cut short lengths of dowelling or when cutting dowelling at an angle, place the dowelling in a wood vise and make the cut with a coping saw (see 2).

Whittling

Round off all edges with a whittling knife (see 3a). Always work away from yourself and use firm, short strokes. Shave off edges and add contours to features such as noses, ears, tail feathers, and so on (see 3b). Use the color section, the photographs at the beginning of the projects, and the detail photographs within the projects as guides to contouring. Finish the contouring by sanding.

Angles are specified to be whittled on the underside of a piece (such as a fin or wing) so that the piece will angle out from the body and add dimension to the animal. Whittle from the dashed line on the pattern (or as described in the directions) towards the star to create either a moderate angle with a specified thickness at the star or an extreme angle that ends in a point. Sand the angle surface flat, as described below.

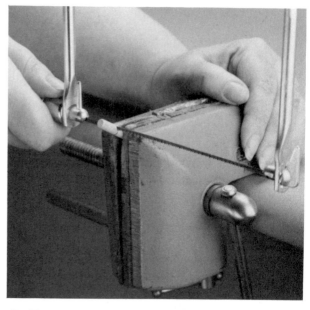

2. To cut short lengths of dowelling, use a coping saw.

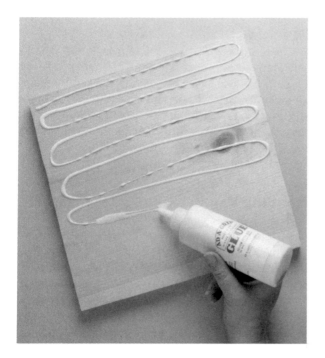

1. To bond wood, run a continuous thin bead of wood glue across the face of each piece.

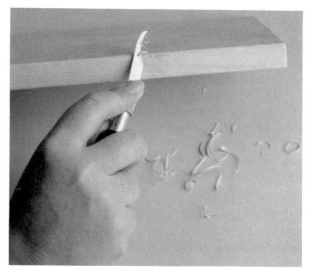

3a. Softening an edge angle with a whittling knife.

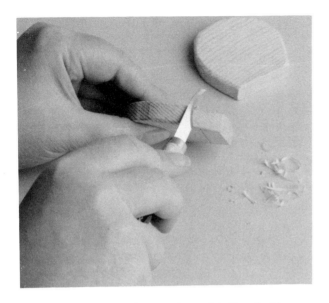

3b. Contouring a piece with a whittling knife.

4. Using a nail set to make an indention at a mark.

Sanding

Thoroughly sand all pieces before assembling. Use medium, then fine-grit, sandpaper, and wipe with a tack cloth to remove the sawdust.

For edges, you can either sand by hand or use the sanding capabilities of your scroll saw. For large areas, use a sanding block fitted with sandpaper or a power palm sander. It's safest to sand small pieces by hand. When sanding whittled angles to make a flat surface for gluing, the easiest method to use is to rub the angle on a piece of sandpaper that has been adhered to a piece of scrap wood or the work surface.

Drilling Holes

For accurate drilling into the edge of a piece, secure the piece in a wood vise so that the marked position of the hole to be drilled is facing up and centered on the width of the vise.

If a hand drill is to be used, make a small indentation at the mark with a hammer and nail set. This will help the drill bit to bite into the wood when you start drilling (see 4). This step isn't necessary if a power drill is used.

Hold the drill perpendicular to the surface to be drilled. Drill the hole to the depth specified in the directions. For accurate hole depths, use a drill stop (see 5).

When drilling into the face of a piece, place the piece on top of scrap lumber and secure both to the work surface with a clamp. To prevent scarring the wood, insert a scrap of ¼ × 5¼ lattice between the clamp and the piece. Drilling through the piece and into the scrap lumber ensures a smooth hole edge on the underside of the piece (see 6).

Gluing and Clamping

Use wood glue whenever you adhere raw wood to raw wood. We recommend that a quick-setting wood glue (such as a cyanoacrylate) be used for those projects that have small pieces or an assembly that is either difficult or impossible to clamp for the length of time it takes regular wood glue to bond. When using a quick-setting wood glue, the pieces can be held firmly together by hand for the few seconds it takes for a permanent bond to form.

5. Drilling a hole with a hand drill and drill stop.

Regular wood glue can be used for adhering axle pegs, dowelling, or applications where clamping is possible. Use spring clamps, C-clamps, bar clamps, or handscrews. Clamping isn't needed when screws or brads are used in addition to glue. Use a waterproof wood glue (as specified) for the tub toys.

Tacky glue, an extra-thick white glue, is used when adhering fabrics and trims to a painted surface or in the rare instances when painted wood is adhered to painted wood.

Countersinking Screws

Projects requiring screws in their assembly have a more finished appearance if time is taken to countersink the screws. After drilling a pilot hole, fit the drill with a countersink bit. Use this bit to drill a cone-shaped hole into the pilot hole to allow the screw head, when fully tightened, to sink about ⅛″ below the surface of the wood. After inserting the screw, fill the hole with paste wood filler, allow to dry, and sand smooth.

Countersinking Brads

Brads should also be countersunk. After driving the brad almost flat to the wood's surface, place a nail set on its head and hammer until the head is ⅟₁₆″ below the surface of the wood. Fill the depression with paste wood filler, allow to dry, and sand smooth.

Cutting Beads in Half

To cut a bead in half, place the bead on the work surface with the hole facing up. Place the center of the whittling knife's blade over the center of the hole, and firmly tap the center top of the blade with a hammer. Sand the cut surface of each bead half smooth by rubbing it on fine-grit sandpaper (see 7).

6. Drilling through two identical parts at once.

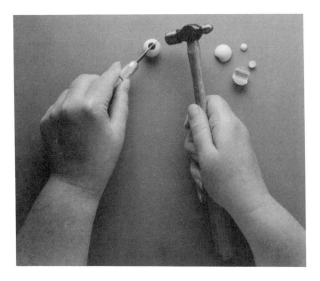

7. *Cutting a bead in half, with the aid of a hammer and a whittling knife.*

Painting and Finishing

When painting, don't allow the paint to flow into pilot holes, axle peg holes, and the like, unless the project's directions instruct otherwise. For the best coverage, apply at least two coats of each color of paint. Allow each color to dry thoroughly between coats or before proceeding to the next step in the directions. For the best paint adhesion, sand lightly between the coats with super-fine-grit sandpaper and wipe with a tack cloth.

When painting and/or assembly is completed, and before adhering trims, apply a protective coating. Unless otherwise specified in the project's Materials list, use a water-base varnish in the type of finish recommended. Apply two or more coats, using super-fine-grit sandpaper to sand lightly between the coats, and then wipe with a tack cloth.

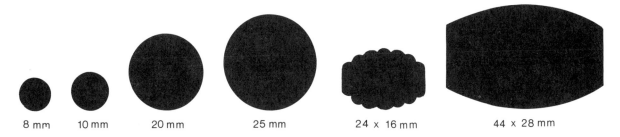

| 8 mm | 10 mm | 20 mm | 25 mm | 24 x 16 mm | 44 x 28 mm |

Bead chart.

PROJECTS

1. Bullfrog

MATERIALS

- 36″ length of ¼ × 5¼ clear pine lattice
- 10″ length of ½ × 5½ clear pine lattice
- One 24 mm × 16 mm, 6-mm hole oval wood bead with seven concentric rings
- Fifteen #20 × ½″ wire brads
- Acrylic paints: medium green, white, black, very dark green, and medium yellow-green
- Acrylic metallic paints: medium blue and gold
- Satin finish

The bullfrog is the largest frog in North America. It lives in the well-vegetated ponds, lakes, and slow-moving streams of eastern and central United States, and it can also be found in parts of Nova Scotia and New Brunswick in Canada. When first hatched, tadpoles are 4 to 6¾ inches long; they may take up to two years to become fully developed frogs. The bullfrog's diet includes insects, crayfish, minnows, and other frogs.

Bullfrog*

1. Cut one body (1–1), two front legs (1–2), and two back legs (1–3) from ½ × 5½ lattice.

2. Cut two front feet (1–4) and two back feet (1–5) from ¼ × 5¼ lattice. The patterns show the orientation of the right feet; the left feet are mirror images.

3. To create the hip angle on the inside of each back leg, whittle a flat surface from the dashed line to the star, so that the thickness at the star is ¼″.

4. Glue the front legs (1–2) to the front feet (1–4) and the back legs (1–3) to the back feet (1–5), as indicated by the dashed lines. Refer to the photograph for the orientation of the feet.

5. Glue the legs to the body, as indicated by the dashed lines in 1–1, making sure that the feet rest flat on the work surface.

6. To make the eyes, cut the bead on either side of the center ring and discard the center ring. Glue the eyes to the sides of the head where indicated by the dots (1–1).

7. Use medium green to paint the body, the largest eye rings, and the top third of the middle and smallest eye rings (see color photo).

8. Use white to paint the lower two-thirds of the middle eye ring on each eye and medium-blue metallic for the lower two-thirds of the smallest eye rings. Paint the inside of the pupil holes of the eyes

---

*Refer to the General Directions for the techniques needed to complete this project.

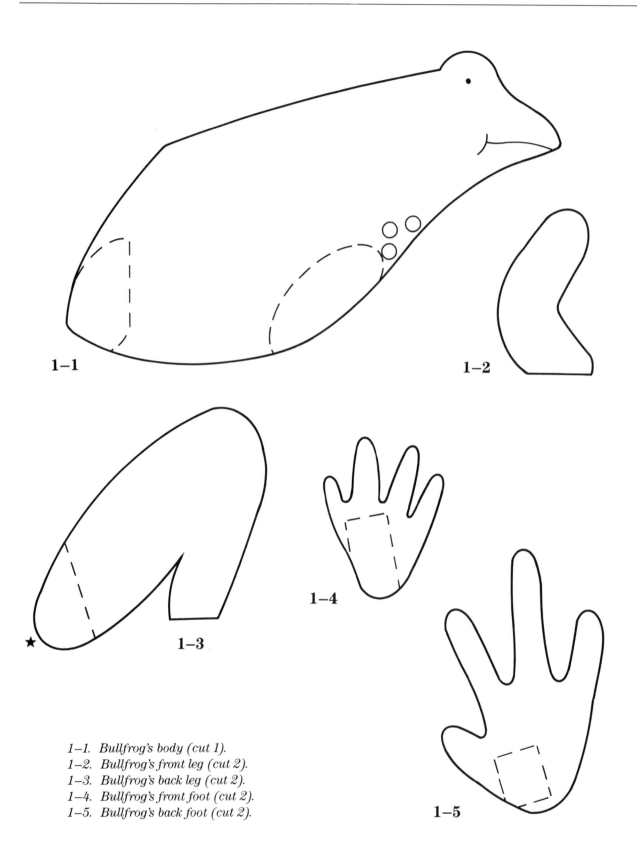

1–1

1–2

1–3

1–4

1–5

1–1. Bullfrog's body (cut 1).
1–2. Bullfrog's front leg (cut 2).
1–3. Bullfrog's back leg (cut 2).
1–4. Bullfrog's front foot (cut 2).
1–5. Bullfrog's back foot (cut 2).

black and paint the mouth black.

9. Use white to highlight the smallest ring of the right eye at 8 o'clock and the left eye at 4 o'clock. Paint the spots on the chest gold metallic, continuing them onto the front edge, as shown in the color photograph.

10. Apply the satin finish.

Lily Pad

1. Cut one lily pad (1–6) from ¼ × 5¼ lattice.

2. Paint the pad very dark green.

3. Apply the satin finish.

Marsh Grass

1. Cut three water bases (1–7) and three sets of marsh grass (1–8) from ¼ × 5¼ lattice.

2. Hammer brads through the water bases where indicated by the stars on 1–7. Apply glue to the bottom of each blade of grass and impale it on a protruding brad. Have the broad face of the grasses parallel with the long sides of the water bases, and vary the arrangement of grasses from one water base to the next.

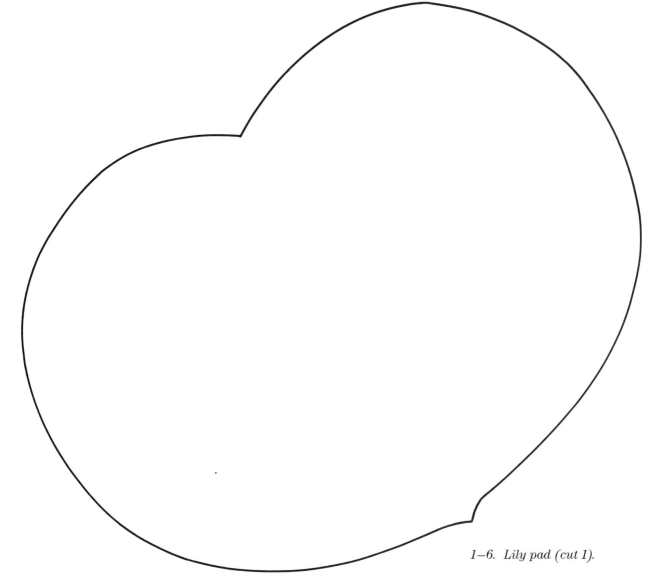

1–6. Lily pad (cut 1).

3. Paint the grasses medium yellow-green and the water bases medium-blue metallic. Use white to paint two or three concentric water ripples halfway around each blade of grass, as shown in the color photograph.

4. Apply the satin finish.

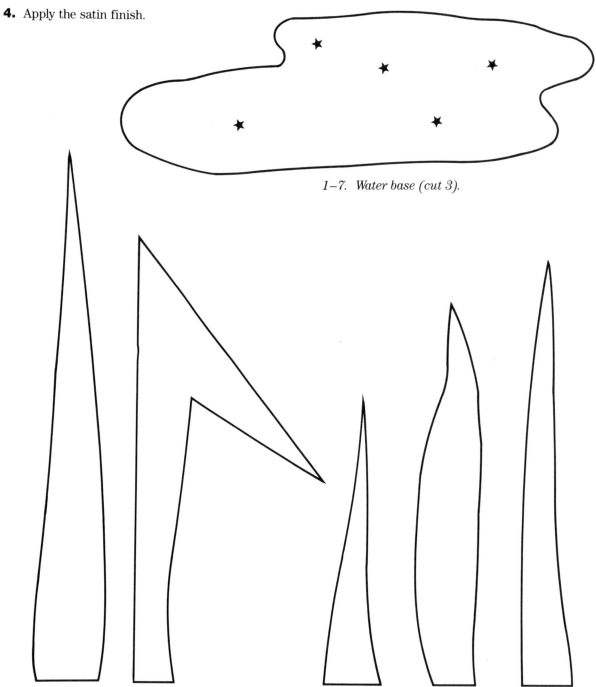

1–7. Water base (cut 3).

1–8. Marsh grass (cut 3 each).

2. Rattlesnakes

MATERIALS

- 2″ length of ¼ × 5¼ clear pine lattice
- 50″ length of ¾″ dowelling

- Two white 8-mm regular-hole round wood beads
- Three white 20-mm large-hole round wood beads
- Two 44 × 28 mm (12-mm hole) oval wood beads
- One round toothpick

- Drill bit: ⅛″

- 2 × 2″ cellulose sponge
- Two 36″ black nylon shoelaces
- Ice pick
- Pointed-tip tweezers
- Small amount of red synthetic suede

- Acrylic paints: light yellow (LY), pale taupe (PT), medium taupe (MT), dark taupe (DT), light red-brown (LRB), dark red-brown (DRB), khaki (K), ecru (E), off-white (OW), medium red-brown, white, and black
- Acrylic metallic paint: medium pink
- Black fine-tip permanent marker
- Satin finish

There are 31 species of these venomous New World reptiles. Rattlesnakes can be found from southern Canada down to northern Argentina and Uruguay. In the United States, they live in every state, except for Maine and Delaware, and are most numerous in the Southwest. Their diet consists mostly of rodents and birds, and, when they can find them, frogs and lizards. (Left) sunbathing rattler and (right) hissing rattler.

Sunbathing Rattler*

1. For the rattle, whittle one end of the uncut dowelling into a 1″-long tapered point, as shown in the photograph above. Then cut a 2¼″ length from the pointed end of the dowelling for the rattle segment.

2. Cut twenty 1″ lengths of dowelling for the body segments.

3. Cut twenty ½ × 1″ rectangles from ¼ × 5¼ lattice, and set aside to use as spacers.

4. Place each body segment in a wood vise with a cut end facing up. Locate the center of the cut end,

and, using the ⅛″ bit, drill a hole through the segment.

5. Secure the rattle segment in a wood vise with the cut end facing up. Using the ⅛″ bit, drill a ¾″-deep hole into the center.

6. Use a 44 × 22 mm bead for the head. Sand the surface if it has a painted or varnished finish.

7. Glue one cut end of a body segment (neck) centered over one hole of the head. Draw a line from the cut end of the neck to the hole at the front of the head. This is the center top of the neck and head. See 2–1 (bottom) for the completed head.

8. Split a 20-mm bead in half for the nose. (Discard one-half.) Sand the cut side so that it covers the other hole of the head. With the 20-mm bead's half-

---

*Refer to the General Directions for the techniques needed to complete this project.

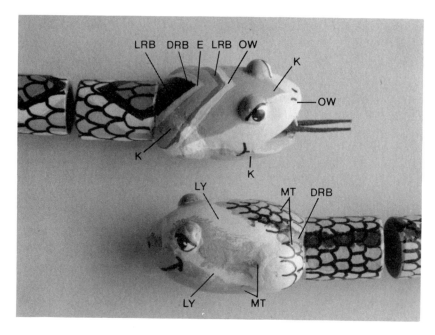

2–1. *Sunbathing rattler (bottom) and hissing rattler (top).*

holes held at right angles to the center line, glue the nose over the hole.

9. Split a 20-mm bead in half for the cheeks. Contour the cut sides by sanding so that they will fit close to the head. With the half-holes held parallel with the center line, glue the cheeks to the sides of the head, ¹⁄₁₆″ from the neck edge.

10. Split an 8-mm bead in half for the eyes. For the position of each eye, make a dot ⅜″ from both sides of the center line and ¾″ from the top of the nose. With the half-holes held parallel with the center line, glue the eyes to the dots.

11. Fill the half-holes and any gaps with paste wood filler, allow to dry, and sand smooth.

12. Transfer body-segment pattern 2–2(a) onto 18 of the body segments, 2–2(b) onto the rattle-end (19th) body segment, and 2–2(c) onto the neck (match the arrow on the pattern with the line indicating the center top of the neck).

13. Referring to the Materials list for the colors, paint the body segments, rattle-end segment, and neck. Use a brush for all colors, except the dark red-brown. For that color, use the sponge to dab on the paint.

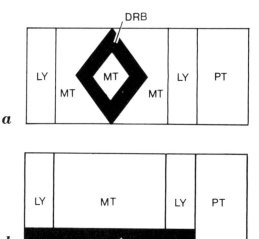

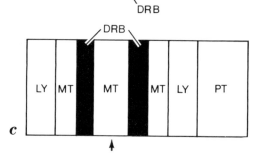

2–2. *Painting patterns for the sunbathing rattler: (a) body segment, (b) rattle-end segment, and (c) neck.*

14. Use dark taupe to paint the cut ends of the 18 body segments and the cut end of the neck. (Paint 1/16″ down into the drilled holes in the cut ends of all the body segments, neck, and rattle.) For the rattle-end body segment, use dark red-brown to paint the cut end adjacent to the dark red-brown sponged area and dark taupe to paint the other cut end.

15. Paint the rattle and its cut end dark red-brown. Use pale taupe to paint a 1/4″-wide × 1 3/8″-long triangle, as shown in the color photograph. Use black to paint six evenly spaced rings around the rattle. Have the first ring 1/4″ from the cut end of the rattle and the last 3/4″ from the tapered end.

16. To paint the head, refer to 2–1 (bottom) and the color photograph. Paint the entire head light yellow, except for the eyes.

17. Now, use the sponge and medium taupe to first overpaint a triangle on the center top of the head, beginning at the sides of the neck and ending with its point 1/4″ above the eyes. Then overpaint patches on the sides of the head, which include the upper half of the eyes. Finally, overpaint the underside of the head, from the neck to the center of the nose.

18. Use the sponge to continue the dark red-brown stripes on the neck onto the head, as shown in 2–1 (bottom).

19. Paint the lower half of the eyes white. Use black to paint the upper and lower eyelids and the pupils. Use white to highlight the right eye at 9 o'clock and the left eye at 3 o'clock.

20. Paint the nostrils and mouth black.

21. Use the black marker to draw the snakeskin pattern (2–3) on the body segments and neck. Either transfer the pattern onto the parts or copy it freehand. Continue the pattern onto the head, as shown in 2–1 (bottom).

22. Apply the satin finish to all parts.

23. Use tacky glue for assembly. Adhere one end of a shoelace into the hole in the cut end of the neck; allow to dry. Place the head on the work surface so that the top of the head faces up. Apply a dab of glue to the shoelace 5/8″ from the cut end of the neck. Draw the free end of the shoelace through a body segment (have the diamond pattern facing up), and place a spacer between the cut end of the neck and the body segment.

24. Repeat for the rest of the body segments, each time applying glue 5/8″ from the cut end of the previously assembled body segment and inserting a spacer. Then position the rattle-end body segment so that its dark taupe cut end faces the previously assembled segment and the pale taupe band (bottom) faces the work surface.

25. Cut the shoelace, leaving a 1″ end. Glue the end into the rattle, insert a spacer, and make sure the pale taupe triangle faces down.

26. Remove the spacers once the glue has dried.

Hissing Rattler

1. Repeat Steps 1 to 6 of the sunbathing rattler. (Reuse the spacers for the hissing rattler.)

2. Referring to the dashed lines on 2–4, draw a line around the middle of the head parallel with the holes (A) and another line 5/16″ above it (B). Divide the head lengthwise into four equal parts through B and A. Mark points 1 and 3. Mark the centerline C as shown on 2–4. To indicate the mouth opening, draw line E from 1 at the hole edge, down to 5 at B, and draw line D from 5 to 3 at the hole edge. Repeat

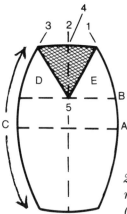

2–4. *Diagram for the hissing rattler's mouth opening (point 4 is behind point 2).*

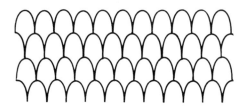

2–3. *Snakeskin pattern.*

lines D and E on the other side of the head. Place the head in a wood vise with the marked end facing up. Use a coping saw to cut the mouth opening, indicated by the shaded area on 2–4. See 2–1 (top) for the completed head.

3. Glue a body segment (neck) over the remaining hole in the other side of the head. Extend line C on the head to the cut end of the neck. This is the center top of the head and neck.

4. Repeat Step 9 of the sunbathing rattler.

5. Split an 8-mm bead in half for the eyes. For the position of each eye, make a dot ⅜″ from both sides of the center line C and ⁹⁄₁₆″ from the front of the head. With the half-holes held parallel with the center line, glue the eyes to the head.

6. Transfer body-segment pattern 2–5(a) onto the 19 body segments and 2–5(b) onto the neck (match the arrow on the pattern with the line indicating the center top of the neck).

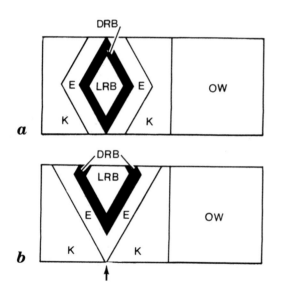

2–5. Painting patterns for the hissing rattler: (a) body segment and (b) neck.

7. Referring to the Materials list for the colors, paint the body segments and neck.

8. Use medium red-brown to paint the cut ends of the body segments and neck. (Paint ¹⁄₁₆″ down into the drilled holes in the cut ends of the body segments, neck, and rattle.)

9. Draw lines to visually divide the rattle lengthwise, from the tip to the cut end, into four equal parts. Paint one part (the underside of the rattle) off-white and the three remaining parts khaki. Using the sponge and light red-brown, overpaint the center khaki part (the top of the rattle). Paint the cut end of the rattle medium red-brown. Using dark red-brown, paint seven evenly spaced rings around the rattle (don't paint into the off-white part). Have the first ring ¼″ from the cut end of the rattle and the last ½″ from the tapered end (see color photo).

10. To paint the head, refer to 2–1 (top) and the color photograph. Complete the light red-brown, dark red-brown, and ecru of the neck's diamond pattern on the back of the head. Outline the pattern with bands of color in the following order: ³⁄₁₆″-wide khaki, ⅛″-wide light red-brown, and ⅛″-wide off-white. Continue the bands onto the underside of the head and end them at the neck.

11. Use khaki to paint the top of the head. Start in the middle of the cheeks, include the upper half of the eyes, and end in a point ¼″ from the center front of the head.

12. Use khaki to paint the bottom of the head. Start at the base of the neck, next to the off-white band. Cover the lower third of the cheeks and along the edge of the lower mouth opening.

13. Paint the rest of the head off-white, except for the eyes.

14. Paint the lower half of the eyes white. Use black to paint the upper eyelids and pupils. Use white to highlight the right eye at 9 o'clock and the left eye at 3 o'clock.

15. Use black to paint the nostrils and the detail at the corners of the mouth. Paint the inside of the mouth medium-pink metallic.

16. Repeat Step 21 of the sunbathing rattler. As shown in 2–1 (top), continue the snakeskin pattern onto the head, but only in the light and dark red-brown areas. Also continue the snakeskin pattern onto the dark red-brown area of the rattle, as shown in the color photograph.

17. Mark for two holes for the fangs on the inside edge of the upper mouth. Mark $\frac{1}{16}''$ from both sides of the center front of the head and $\frac{1}{16}''$ in from the edge of the mouth. Use the ice pick to make $\frac{1}{16}''$-deep holes.

18. For the fangs, use white to paint $\frac{1}{2}''$ down both tips of the toothpick. Cut two $\frac{5}{16}''$ tips from the toothpick. Hold the fangs with tweezers, and use tacky glue to adhere the cut ends into the holes.

19. Repeat Steps 22 to 26 of the sunbathing rattler. (Disregard the directions for the rattle-end body segment, and have the off-white part of the rattle face down when assembling.)

20. Cut one tongue (2–6) from red synthetic suede. Hold the tongue with tweezers, and use tacky glue to adhere its straight end to the lower back of the throat.

2–6. Hissing rattler's tongue pattern (cut 1).

3. Wood Duck Paddle Toys

The male wood duck is the most strikingly colored of all American water fowl and the female is the most elegant. Wood ducks are found in east and central North America, from southern Canada to Florida. Wood ducks live in wooded swamps, rivers, and ponds. They nest in tree cavities and return to the same nest every year.

Female Wood Duck*

1. Cut one body (3–1) and one platform (3–2) from ½ × 5½ lattice.

2. Cut two paddles (3–3), two wings (3–4), two small waves (3–5), and two large waves (3–6) from ¼ × 5¼ lattice. The wing pattern shows the orientation of the left wing; the right wing is a mirror image.

3. Using the ¹⁄₁₆″ bit, drill ¼″-deep pilot holes into the lower edge of the body where indicated by the arrows on 3–1.

4. Using the ¹⁄₁₆″ bit, drill pilot holes through the platform where indicated by the circles on 3–2.

5. Using the ⁷⁄₃₂″ bit, drill ¾″-deep peg holes into the center back of each platform arm where indicated by the arrows on 3–2.

*Refer to the General Directions for the techniques needed to complete this project.

6. Glue the axle pegs into the holes in the platform arms. To assemble the paddles, apply a small amount of glue to the inside edge of each paddle slot and slip one slot into the other.

7. To create the angle on the inside of each wing (3–4), whittle a flat surface from the dashed line to the star so that the thickness at the star is ⅛″.

8. Glue the wing angles to the body, where indicated by the dashed lines on 3–1 (see color photo for reference).

9. Cut a 10-mm bead in half for the eyes. With the half-holes held horizontally, glue the eyes to the sides of the head where indicated by the dashed circles on 3–1.

10. Glue the small and large waves to the platform where indicated by the dashed lines on 3–2.

11. Apply glue to the bottom edge of the duck. Secure it to the platform with screws inserted from the underside of the platform.

12. Paint the body as shown on 3–1 and the color photograph. (See the Materials list for the colors.) Extend the colors onto the edge surfaces. Paint the wings as shown on 3–4 (the labels F and M on the pattern indicate the colors to be used for the female and male ducks). See the steps below for additional painting directions.

13. Extend the white and light mocha-brown areas at the front of the head ⅛″ onto both sides of the edge surface. Paint the center of the edge surface, from the forehead to the tip of the bill, medium grey-green.

14. Use black to paint the underside of the bill, from the edge of the white patch at the jaw to the tip of the bill.

15. Use dark yellow to paint a ring around the inner third of each eye (closest to the head) and white to paint a ring around the middle third (see color photo). For the pupils, paint the rest of the eyes black. Using white, highlight the right eye at 8 o'clock and the left eye at 4 o'clock.

16. Paint the platform and paddle assembly light blue.

17. Apply the high-gloss waterproof finish to all parts.

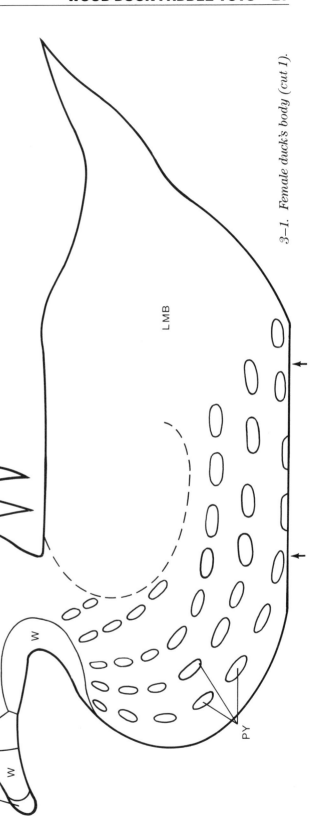

3–1. Female duck's body (cut 1).

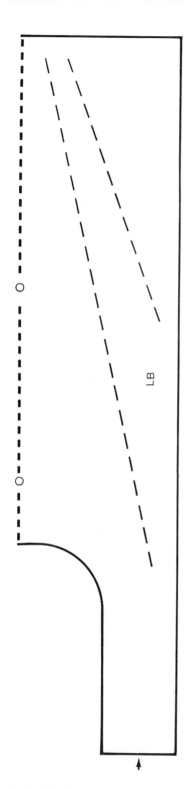

3–2. Half-pattern for the platform (cut 1 platform for each duck).

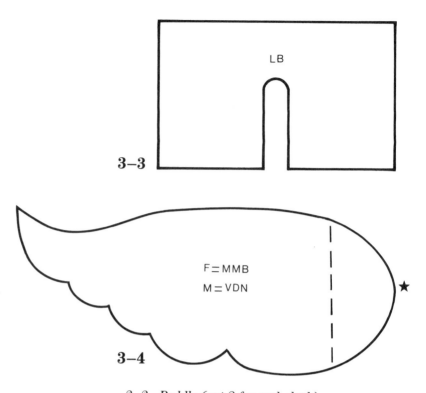

3–3. Paddle (cut 2 for each duck).
3–4. Female and male ducks' wing (cut 2 for each).

18. Slip the rubber band around the paddles, and then slip its ends over the pegs.

Male Wood Duck

1. Repeat Steps 1 to 12 of the female wood duck, using the pattern for the male wood duck (3–7) instead of 3–1. See the steps below for additional painting instructions.

2. Extend the white and terra-cotta areas on the front of the head ¹⁄₁₆″ onto both sides of the front edge surfaces. Use black to paint the center of the edge surface, from the forehead to the tip of the bill.

3. Use black to paint the underside of the bill, from the edge of the white patch at the jaw to the tip of the bill.

4. Use terra cotta to paint a ring for the inner circle of each eye (see color photo). For the pupils, paint the rest of the eyes black.

5. Repeat Steps 16 to 18 of the female wood duck.

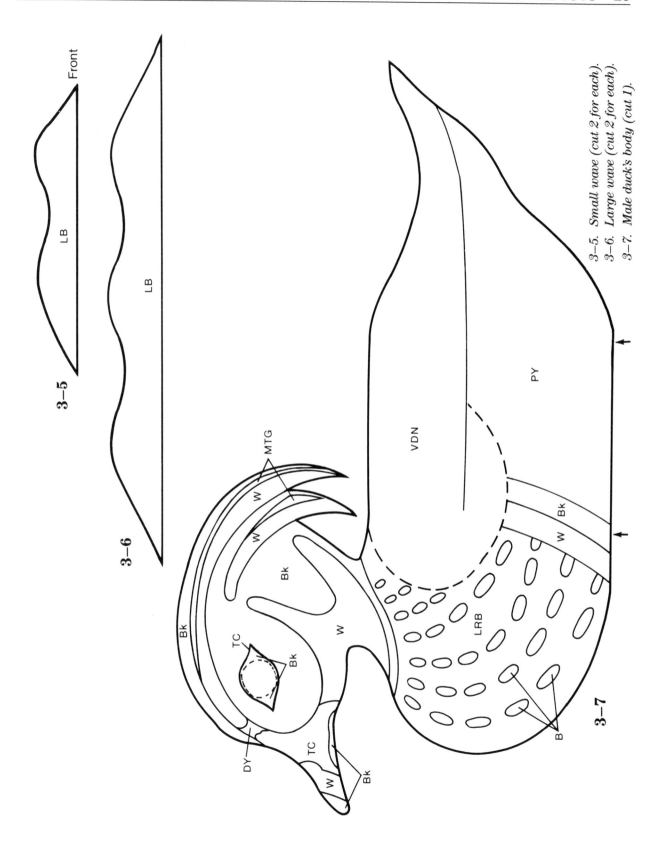

Front

3–5

3–6

LB

LB

3–7

MTG

W

W

Bk

W

Bk

TC

Bk

DY

TC

W

Bk

VDN

LRB

W

Bk

PY

B

3–5. *Small wave (cut 2 for each).*
3–6. *Large wave (cut 2 for each).*
3–7. *Male duck's body (cut 1).*

4. Whale and Dolphin Mobile

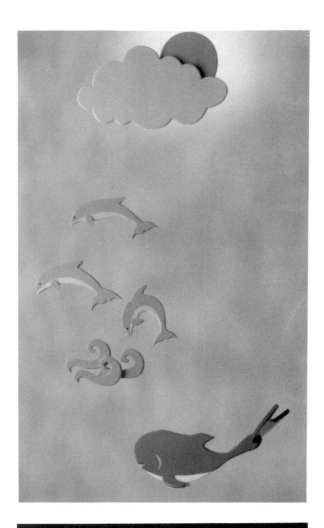

Whales and dolphins are magnificent denizens of the deep who swim the oceans and seas of the world. There are two kinds of whales: baleen and toothed. Baleen is a flexible curtain of whalebone, which hangs from the upper jaw and acts as a strainer to separate water from plankton and other tiny marine animals that these whales eat. The blue, humpback, finback, and grey are all baleen whales. Measuring up to 113 feet in length and weighing an estimated 200 tons, the blue whale is the largest mammal to have ever roamed the oceans.

The sperm whale, which can grow to 60 feet in length, is the largest of the toothed whales. It eats fish and giant squid, dives a half mile (.8 km) deep in search of prey, and can stay submerged for 40 minutes. The dolphin is the smallest toothed whale. Ranging in length from 7 to 12 feet, and weighing up to 200 pounds (91 kg), dolphins live on fish and squid and travel in groups of 50 to 1,000 individuals.

MATERIALS

- 40″ length of ¼ × 5¼ clear pine lattice
- Three ice-cream sticks
- One round toothpick
- 48½″ length of 5-lb. test nylon fishing line
- #18 pointed sewing needle
- Ice pick
- Acrylic paints: dark grey, white, light grey, black, light blue, and medium yellow
- Satin finish

Whale*

1. Cut one body (4–1), one tail (4–2), and two flippers (4–3) from ¼ × 5¼ lattice.

2. Glue the tail into the notch in the body.

3. Whittle the underside of each flipper to a 45° angle, working from the dashed line to the straight edge.

4. Glue the flipper angles to the sides of the body where indicated by the dashed lines on 4–1. Have the tips of the flippers pointed towards the back of the whale, as shown in the photograph.

5. Insert the needle into the center of the mouth where indicated by the arrow in 4–1, and make a ⅛″-deep hole.

---

*Refer to the General Directions for the techniques needed to complete this project.

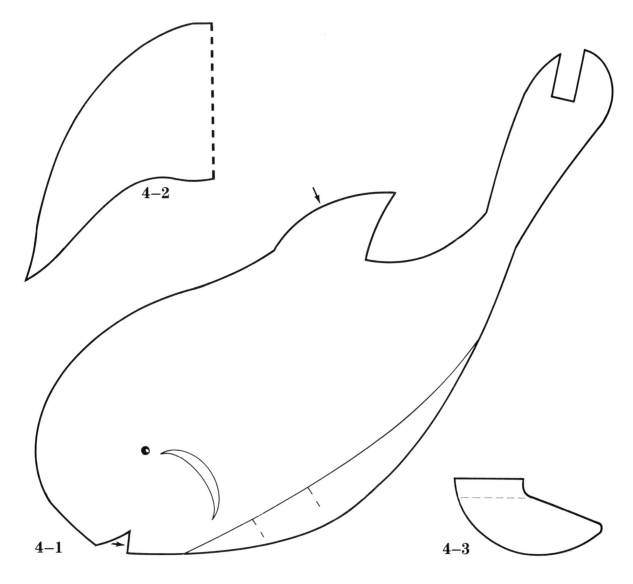

4–1. Whale's body (cut 1).
4–2. Half-pattern for the whale's tail (cut 1).
4–3. Whale's flipper (cut 2).

6. Cut a ¼″ length from one end of the toothpick for the tooth. Glue the pointed end of the tooth into the hole in the mouth.

7. Use dark grey to paint the upper body, the tail, and the tops and edges of the flippers (see color photo). Use white to paint the lower body, the undersides of the flippers, and the tooth. Paint the face markings light grey, the eyes black, and the eye highlights white.

8. Apply the satin finish.

9. Insert the needle into the dorsal fin where indicated by the arrow in 4–1, and make a ⅛″-deep hole.

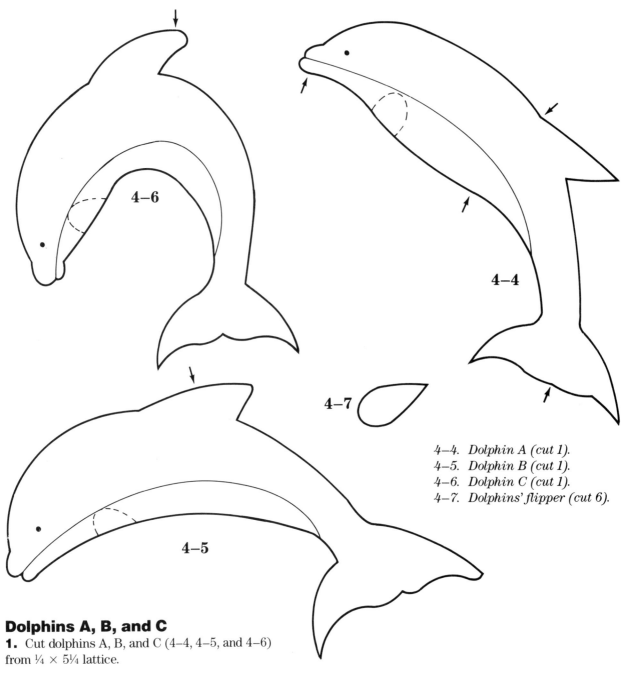

4–6

4–4

4–7

4–5

4–4. Dolphin A (cut 1).
4–5. Dolphin B (cut 1).
4–6. Dolphin C (cut 1).
4–7. Dolphins' flipper (cut 6).

Dolphins A, B, and C

1. Cut dolphins A, B, and C (4–4, 4–5, and 4–6) from ¼ × 5¼ lattice.

2. Cut six flippers (4–7) from the rounded ends of three ice-cream sticks.

3. Glue the flippers to the sides of the dolphins where indicated by the dashed lines on the patterns.

4. Paint the upper bodies and the tops and edges of the flippers light grey. Use white to paint the lower bodies and the undersides of the flippers. Paint the eyes black.

5. Apply the satin finish.

6. Using the needle, make ⅛"-deep holes where indicated by the arrows on the patterns.

Toucan (see pp. 51–57); Scarlet Macaw (see pp. 42–50); and Pink Cockatoo (see pp. 121–125). Toucans live in Central and South America and nest in tree cavities. They are fruit eaters. Macaws live in South America, Mexico, and Trinidad. They eat nuts, seeds, and fruit. The Pink Cockatoo, an Australian native, is a forest-dweller that eats seeds, roots, and tubers, which it digs up with its beak.

Lion Pull Toy (see pp. 64–69). Lions inhabit the grassy plains and woodlands of Africa. They may grow up to 8 feet in length.

Wood Duck Paddle Toys (see pp. 26–29). Left, female; right, male. Wood ducks live in wooded swamps, rivers, and ponds in eastern North America.

Giraffe Pull Toy (see pp. 70–77). Foreground, female; standing, male. Giraffes live on the grasslands of Africa. The male, at 19 feet, is the tallest animal on earth. Giraffes eat twigs, bark, and leaves.

B

Koalas (see pp. 107–110). Koalas are slow-moving animals. They live in the forests of eastern Australia. Their diet consists solely of eucalyptus leaves and bark.

Rattlesnakes (see pp. 21–25). Left, sunbathing snake; right, hissing snake. Rattlesnakes are venomous New World reptiles. There are over 31 species of rattlesnake.

Goldfish Bowl (see pp. 82–88). Goldfish, domesticated by the Chinese over 1,000 years ago, are native to East Asia. In the wild they can grow to a length of 12 inches.

American Alligator (see pp. 35–38) and Pond Slider Turtles (see pp. 39–41). The American alligator is the largest reptile in North America. It lives in swamps, lakes, bayous, and marshes. Pond slider turtles inhabit ponds, shallow streams and slow-moving rivers from the southern United States south to Brazil. They range in length from 5 to 12 inches.

Greater Pandas (see pp. 89–93). Pandas live only in the remote forests of the People's Republic of China. Their diet consists mainly of bamboo. Although very small at birth, they can grow to 300 lbs (136 kg).

Shark School Paddle Toy (see pp. 118–120). Sharks have been on earth for more than 350 million years. They live in the tropical and temperate waters of the world. Their length ranges from 1 to 60 feet.

Tiger Hobbyhorse (see pp. 94–97) and Zebra Hobbyhorse (see pp. 78–81). Tigers are solitary, mostly nocturnal Asian animals that eat deer, wild cattle, and wild pigs. They may grow to 9 feet in length. Zebras live in the plains, hillsides, and rocky slopes of Africa. No two zebras have exactly the same stripe pattern.

Tropical Fish Aquarium (see pp. 111–117). Millions of beautiful tropical fish live in Australia's Great Barrier Reef.

Whale and Dolphin Mobile (see pp. 30–34). Some whales have teeth. Others have baleen, a bony strainer that catches the tiny marine animals on which they feed. Dolphins are the smallest toothed whales.

Spider Monkeys (see pp. 58–63). Spider monkeys are agile treetop dwellers that can be found in the forests from Mexico to Brazil. They feed on fruit, nuts, flowers, and buds.

G

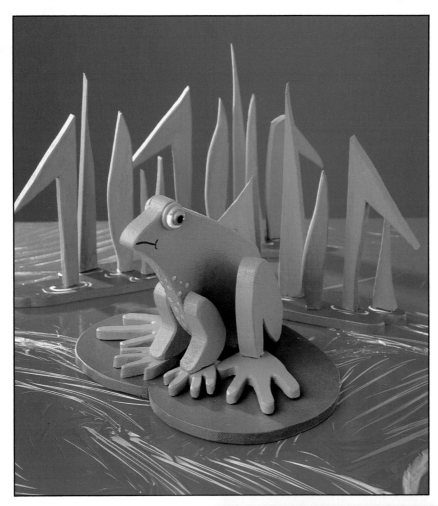

Bullfrog (see pp. 17–20). The bullfrog is the largest frog in North America, sometimes growing to 6¾ inches in length. Bullfrogs eat insects, crayfish, minnows, and other frogs.

Asian Elephant Pull Toy (see pp. 98–106). Elephants are the largest living land animals. A baby elephant may weigh 200 lbs (91 kg) at birth. Asian elephants have been used as work animals for thousands of years.

Waves

1. Cut three waves (4–8) from ¼ × 5¼ lattice.

2. Glue the waves together, as shown in the photograph.

3. Paint the waves light blue.

4. Apply the satin finish.

5. Insert the needle into the uppermost wave where indicated by the arrow on 4–8, and make a ⅛″-deep hole.

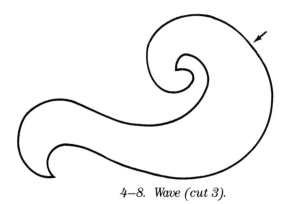

4–8. Wave (cut 3).

Sun and Cloud

1. Cut one sun (4–9) and one cloud (4–10) from ¼ × 5¼ lattice.

2. Glue the sun behind the cloud where indicated by the dashed line on 4–10.

3. Paint the sun medium yellow and the cloud white.

4. Apply the satin finish.

5. Insert the needle where indicated by the two bottom arrows on 4–10, and make ⅛″-deep holes.

6. Insert the ice pick where indicated by the top arrow on 4–10, and make a ⅛″-deep hole.

Assembly

1. After cutting the fishing line to the lengths described below, tie five consecutive knots at each end. Trim each end close to the outermost knot. Use tacky glue to adhere the knotted ends into the holes indicated.

2. Cut a 19½″ length of fishing line. Glue one end into the dorsal-fin hole in the whale and the opposite end into the bottom right hole in the cloud.

3. Cut a 6″ length of fishing line. Glue one end into the top hole in dolphin A and the opposite end into the bottom left hole in the cloud.

4. Cut a 3½″ length of fishing line. Glue one end into the top hole in dolphin B and the opposite end into the chin hole in dolphin A.

5. Cut a 4½″ length of fishing line. Glue one end into the top hole in dolphin C and the opposite end into the tail hole in dolphin A.

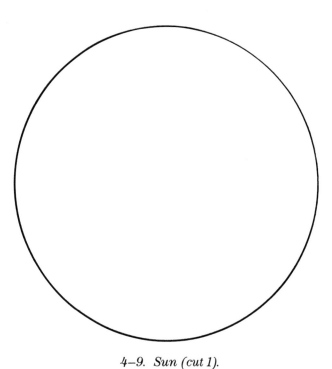

4–9. Sun (cut 1).

6. Cut an 8½" length of fishing line. Glue one end into the hole in the top wave and the opposite end into the lower body hole in dolphin A.

7. For the hanger, cut a 6½" length of fishing line. With both ends together and even, make five consecutive knots. Trim the ends of the hanger close to the last knot. Glue the knotted end into the top hole in the cloud.

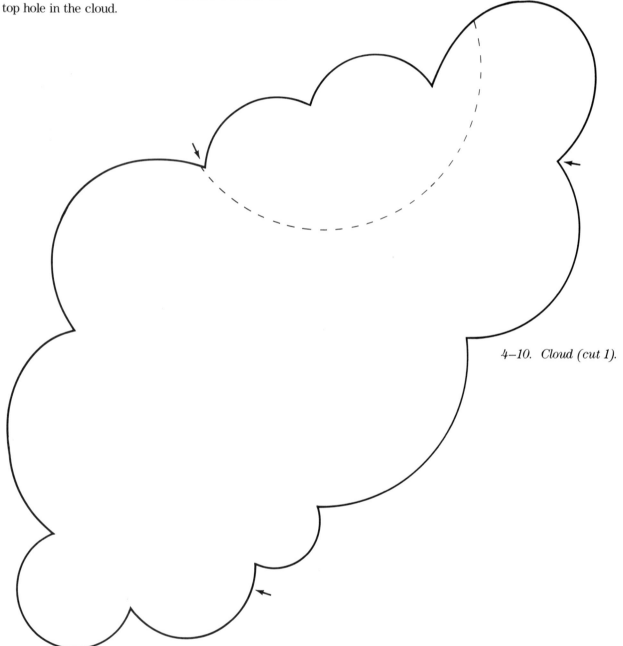

4–10. Cloud (cut 1).

5. American Alligator

MATERIALS

- 24″ length of ¼ × 1⅜ clear pine lattice
- 6″ length of ¼ × 5¼ clear pine lattice
- 15″ length of ½ × 5½ clear pine lattice

- Four 1¼″-long × ¼″-diameter wooden axle pegs
- 35 round toothpicks
- One white 8-mm regular-hole round wood bead
- One white 20-mm large-hole round wood bead

- Drill bits: ¹⁄₁₆″ and ⁷⁄₃₂″

- Pointed-tip tweezers

- Acrylic paints: dark salmon pink, ecru, very dark grey-green, white, and black
- High-gloss finish

Native only to the United States and measuring 6 to 19 feet long, American alligators are the largest reptiles in North America. Alligators are found in swamps, lakes, bayous, and marshes from the coast of North Carolina, south to the Florida Keys, and west along the coastal plain to southern Texas. They eat fish, small mammals, birds, turtles, snakes, and frogs. Females lay up to 60 eggs in a mud nest, and, after nine weeks, the 10-inch hatchlings emerge. Surprisingly, a baby alligator stays with its mother until it is one to three years old!

Alligator*

1. Cut two 15″ lengths of ½ × 5½ lattice, and glue the faces together to make a bonded piece with a finished size of 15″ × 5⁷⁄₁₆″ × ¹⁵⁄₁₆″. Cut one body (5–1) from the bonded wood.

2. Cut one upper head (5–2), two front legs (5–3), and two back legs (5–4) from ½ × 5½ lattice.

3. Cut one tongue (5–5), two front feet (5–6), and two back feet (5–7) from ¼ × 5¼ lattice. The feet patterns show the orientation of the right feet; the left feet are mirror images.

4. Cut two jaw wedges (5–8) and four back scales (5–9) from ¼ × 1⅜ lattice.

5. At each arrow on the body (5–1), mark ⅝″ down from the top edge for the axle peg holes. Using the ⁷⁄₃₂″ bit, drill ½″-deep holes. Then drill axle peg holes, where indicated by the stars, through the front and back legs (5–3 and 5–4).

---

*Refer to the General Directions for the techniques needed to complete this project.

6. Cut the lower jaw and lower jaw angle at the front of the body (5–1), as diagrammed in 5–10. Discard the shaded area.

7. Across the underside of the upper head (5–2), draw a line ½″ from and parallel with the straight edge. Whittle a 45° angle, working from the line to the straight edge.

8. Starting at the center of the lower jaw (5–1), mark for 35 tooth holes (one in the middle and 17 on each side), spaced ⅛″ in from the edge and ⅛″ apart. Repeat for the underside of the upper head (5–2). Using the ¹⁄₁₆″ bit, drill ⅛″-deep holes.

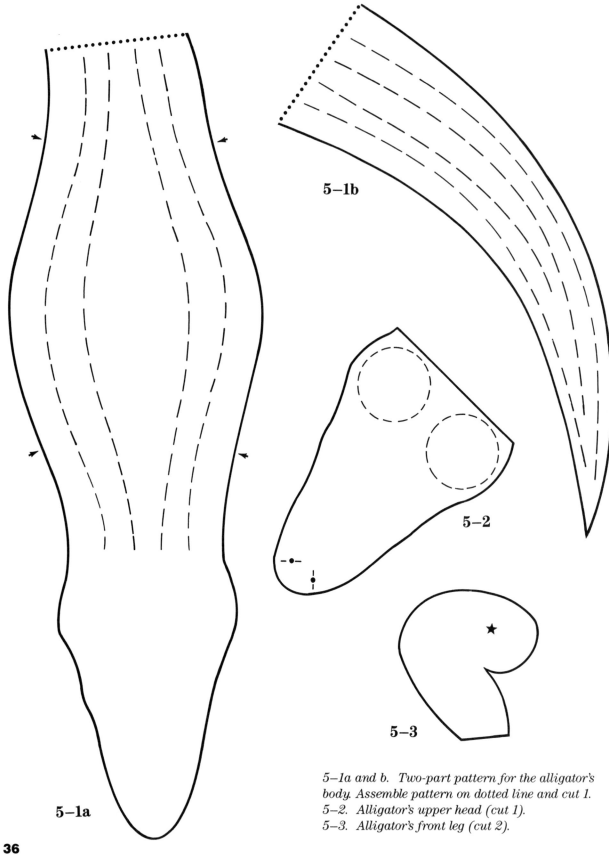

5—1b

5—1a

5—2

5—3

5—1a and b. Two-part pattern for the alligator's body. Assemble pattern on dotted line and cut 1.
5—2. Alligator's upper head (cut 1).
5—3. Alligator's front leg (cut 2).

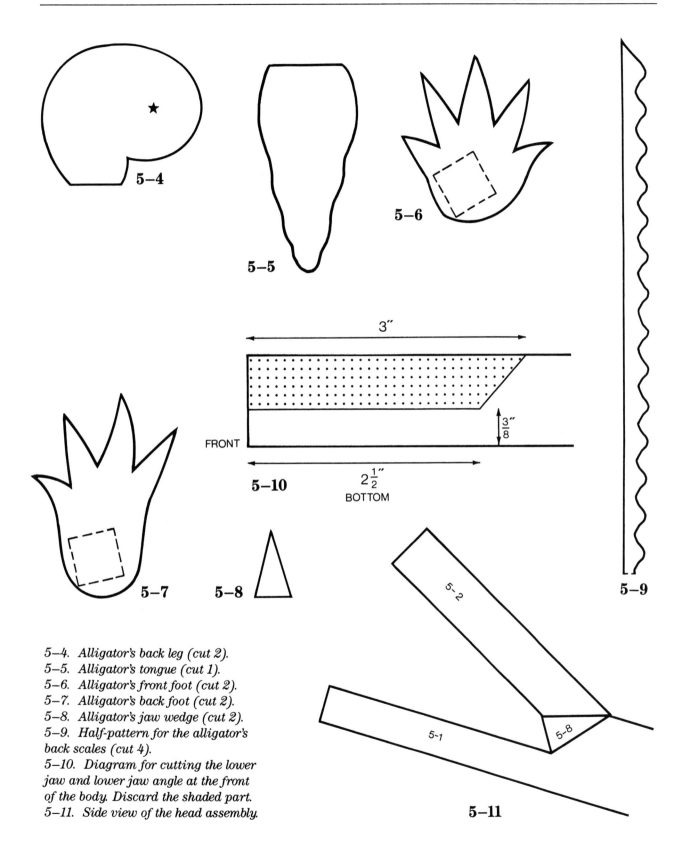

3″

FRONT

$\frac{3}{8}$″

5–10

$2\frac{1}{2}$″
BOTTOM

5–4. *Alligator's back leg (cut 2).*
5–5. *Alligator's tongue (cut 1).*
5–6. *Alligator's front foot (cut 2).*
5–7. *Alligator's back foot (cut 2).*
5–8. *Alligator's jaw wedge (cut 2).*
5–9. *Half-pattern for the alligator's back scales (cut 4).*
5–10. *Diagram for cutting the lower jaw and lower jaw angle at the front of the body. Discard the shaded part.*
5–11. *Side view of the head assembly.*

9. Glue the tongue (5–5) to the lower jaw, with its tip ⅜″ from the front of the jaw and centered from side to side.

10. To assemble the head as shown in 5–11, first glue the jaw wedges (5–8) to the lower jaw angles (5–1). Then glue the angle on the underside of the upper head (5–2) to the jaw wedges. Fill any gaps with paste wood filler, allow to dry, and sand smooth.

11. Split the 20-mm bead in half for the eyes. With the half-holes parallel with the back of the upper head, glue the eyes to the upper head where indicated by the dashed circles on 5–2. Fill the half-holes with paste wood filler, allow to dry, and sand smooth.

12. Split the 8-mm bead in half for the nostrils. With the half holes angled as shown by the dashed lines on 5–2, glue the nostrils to the upper head where indicated by the dots. Fill the rear half-holes only with paste wood filler, allow to dry, and sand smooth.

13. Starting at the base of the upper head, glue the back scales (5–9) to the body where indicated by the dashed lines on 5–1 and as shown in the photograph at the beginning of the project. To accommodate curves, cut the scales into shorter lengths.

14. Glue the front legs (5–3) to the front feet (5–6) and the back legs (5–4) to the back feet (5–7) where indicated by the dashed lines.

15. Paint the inside of the mouth and the tongue dark salmon-pink. Paint the underbody ecru and the edge details (as shown in 5–12) very dark grey-green. Use very dark grey-green to paint the rest of the body, head, back of the eyes (as shown in 5–13), nose, legs, feet, and axle peg caps.

16. As shown in 5–13, paint the irises black with white pupils and white on either side of the irises. Use black to paint the upper-eyelid lines.

17. For the teeth, use white to paint ⅜″ down both tips of each toothpick. Cut ⁵⁄₁₆″ tips from the toothpicks. Using tweezers to hold the teeth, adhere

5–12. Alligator's underbody.

5–13. Alligator's face.

the cut ends into the holes in the mouth with tacky glue.

18. Apply the high-gloss finish to all parts.

19. To attach each leg, apply a small amount of glue into a peg hole in the body. Insert an axle peg through the peg hole in a corresponding leg and then into the glued peg hole in the body. The legs should be able to move up and down.

6. Pond Slider Turtles

MATERIALS

- 10″ length of ¼ × 2⅝ clear pine lattice
- 6″ length of ½ × 3½ clear pine lattice
- 20″ length of 1 × 10 clear pine

- One white 8-mm regular-hole round wood bead
- Two white 10-mm regular-hole round wood beads

- Acrylic paints: dark green, pale yellow, white, black, bright red, and light moss-green
- High-gloss finish

Father and Mother Turtles*

The following directions are for one turtle. The second large turtle is made in the same manner as this one.

1. Cut two 7″ lengths of 1 × 10 pine and glue the faces together to make a bonded piece with a finished size of 7″ × 9¼″ × 1½″. Cut one shell (6–1) from the bonded wood. (Reserve the remainder for the second turtle.)

2. Cut one head (6–2) and one underbody (6–3) from 1 × 10 pine.

3. Cut four feet (6–4) and one tail (6–5) from ¼ × 2⅝ lattice.

4. Glue the underbody (6–3) to the bottom of the shell between the squares shown on 6–1 and centered from side to side.

5. Glue the head and tail into the spaces between the shell and underbody, as shown in the photograph at the beginning of the project and in 6–6.

6. Glue the feet to the sides of the underbody where indicated by the dashed lines on 6–3. Have the front feet point forwards and the back feet point backwards.

7. Split a 10-mm bead in half for the eyes. With the half-holes held horizontal, glue the eyes to the sides of head where indicated by the dots on 6–2.

8. Split the 8-mm bead in half for the nose.

---

*Refer to the General Directions for the techniques needed to complete this project.

Called "dime-store" turtles, millions of pond sliders have been raised on turtle farms to be sold as pets. In the wild, they inhabit sluggish rivers, shallow streams, swamps, and ponds, from southeast Virginia to northern Florida, west to New Mexico, and south to Brazil. They range in length from 5 to 12 inches. They love to bask in the sun and are often seen stacked one upon another on a log. Like most turtles, the young eat insects, crustaceans, mollusks, and tadpoles, and turn to an all-plant diet as they mature.

(Reserve one-half for the other turtle.) With the half-holes held vertical, glue the nose to the front of the head where indicated by the arrow on 6–2.

9. Paint the head, shell, tail, and feet dark green. Use pale yellow to paint the underbody and the underside of the shell. Use bright red to paint the triangular patches on the sides of the head.

10. Paint the shell details light moss-green (see color photo). Continue the shell details onto the top edge, as shown in the photograph at the beginning of the project. (The shell details on the rear top edge are a mirror image of the details on the front top edge.)

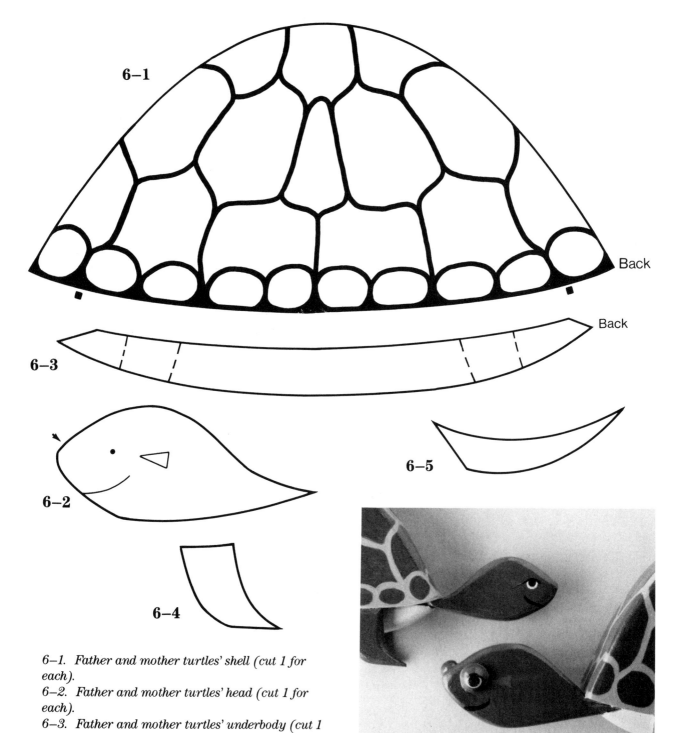

6-1

Back

Back

6-3

6-5

6-2

6-4

6-1. *Father and mother turtles' shell (cut 1 for each).*

6-2. *Father and mother turtles' head (cut 1 for each).*

6-3. *Father and mother turtles' underbody (cut 1 for each).*

6-4. *Father and mother turtles' foot (cut 4 for each).*

6-5. *Father and mother turtles' tail (cut 1 for each).*

6-6. *Parent and baby turtles' faces.*

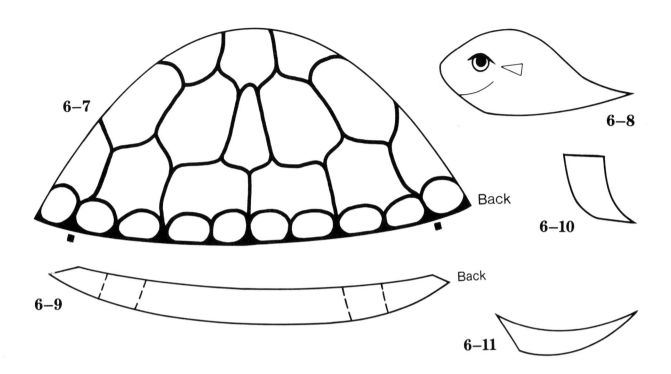

6–7

6–8

Back

6–10

Back

6–9

6–11

11. As shown in 6–6, use dark green to paint the upper eyelids and the bases of the eyes. Paint the eye rings white. Use black to paint the pupils, upper-eyelid lines, and mouth. Extend the mouth onto the front edge of the face in an inverted U.

12. Apply the high-gloss finish.

Baby Turtle

1. Cut one shell (6–7) from 1 × 10 pine.

2. Cut one head (6–8) and one underbody (6–9) from ½ × 3½ lattice.

3. Cut four feet (6–10) and one tail (6–11) from ¼ × 2⅝ lattice.

6–7. Baby turtle's shell (cut 1).
6–8. Baby turtle's head (cut 1).
6–9. Baby turtle's underbody (cut 1).
6–10. Baby turtle's foot (cut 4).
6–11. Baby turtle's tail (cut 1).

4. Repeat Steps 4, 5, 6, 9, and 10 of the father and mother turtles.

5. Paint the eyelid lines and the pupils black, as shown in 6–6. Use white to paint the eye rings.

6. Apply the high-gloss finish.

7. Scarlet Macaw

MATERIALS

- 70" length of ¼ × 5¼ clear pine lattice
- 2" length of ½ × 3½ clear pine lattice
- 12" length of 1 × 6 clear pine
- 12" length of 1 × 10 clear pine
- 18" length of ⅜" dowelling
- 5" length of ⅝" dowelling
- One white 10-mm regular-hole round wood bead

- Drill bits: ¼" and ⅜"

- One 7"-long yellow feather fluff
- 2"-long feather fluffs: two blue, 12 red, and 12 yellow
- 2 × 2 cellulose sponge

- Acrylic paints: pale blue-grey (PBG), charcoal grey (CG), bright red (BR), black (B), white (W), off-white (OW), medium yellow (MY), dark ultramarine (DU), dark red-brown, very dark grey-green, and light yellow-green
- High-gloss finish

Scarlet macaws are native to the tropical areas of South America, Mexico, and Trinidad. They live in treetops near the meandering rivers of rain forests and open woodlands. Scarlet macaws average 33 inches in length and eat a diet consisting of nuts, seeds, and fruit. They move about in large flocks made up of several dozen pairs and make their presence known with ear-splitting, raucous calls.

Macaw*

1. Cut one body (7–1) from 1 × 6 pine.

2. Cut one beak (7–2) from ½ × 3½ lattice.

3. Cut two legs (7–3), two red tail feathers (7–4), and one blue tail feather (7–5) from ¼ × 5¼ lattice. Figures 7–3 and 7–4 show the orientation of the right leg and the right red tail feather; the left leg and the left red tail feather are mirror images.

---

*Refer to the General Directions for the techniques needed to complete this project.

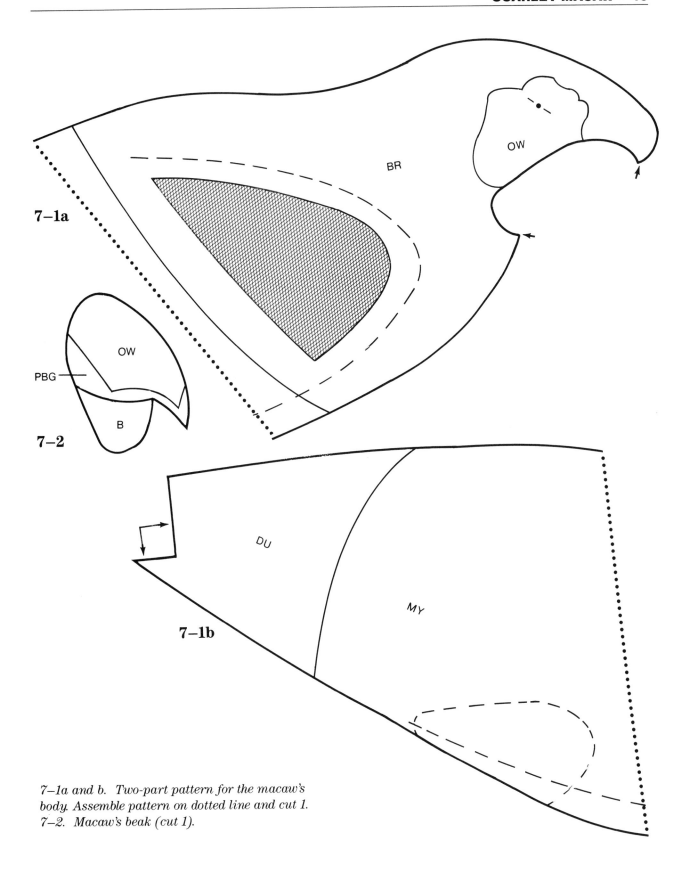

7–1a

7–2

OW

PBG

B

BR

OW

7–1b

DU

MY

7–1a and b. *Two-part pattern for the macaw's
body. Assemble pattern on dotted line and cut 1.*
7–2. *Macaw's beak (cut 1).*

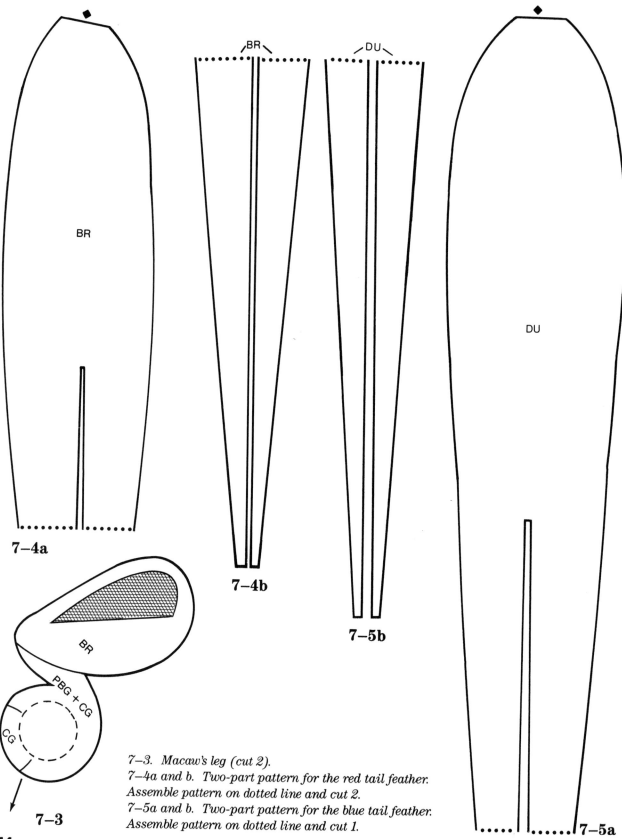

7–4a

7–4b

7–5b

BR

PBG + CG

CG

7–3

7–5a

DU

7–3. *Macaw's leg (cut 2).*
7–4a and b. *Two-part pattern for the red tail feather.*
Assemble pattern on dotted line and cut 2.
7–5a and b. *Two-part pattern for the blue tail feather.*
Assemble pattern on dotted line and cut 1.

4. Cut two each of the bottom (7–6), middle (7–7), and top (7–8) wings from ¼ × 5¼ lattice. The patterns show the orientation of the right wings; the left wings are mirror images. After cutting out and before transferring the painting lines, gluing areas, and dashed lines, mark the upper surface of each piece as right wing or left wing.

5. Transfer the painting lines on 7–6 and 7–7 to both sides of the bottom and middle wings, flopping the pattern over when needed.

6. Transfer the dashed line and tinted gluing area on 7–6 to the undersides of the bottom wings.

7. Transfer the tinted gluing area pattern (7–9) to the upper surfaces of the bottom wings (7–6), both sides of the middle wings (7–7), and the undersides of the top wings (7–8). Match the wing outline on 7–9 with the upper edge of the cut pieces, flopping the pattern over when needed.

8. Split the 10-mm bead in half for the eyes. With the half-holes angled as shown by the dashed line on 7–1, glue the eyes to the head where indicated by the dots. Fill the half-holes with paste wood filler, allow to dry, and sand smooth.

9. Glue the beak (7–2) to the front of the head between the arrows on 7–1.

10. Glue the legs (7–3) to the sides of the body where indicated by the small curved dashed lines on 7–1.

11. Cut a length of ⅝″ dowelling that will fit snugly between the feet without bowing out the legs. (This is the middle-perch segment.) Don't glue it yet, however. Cut two 1⅛″ lengths of ⅝″ dowelling for the outer-perch segments.

12. Using the ¼″ bit, drill a ⅜″-deep hole for the perch support in the center of the length of the middle-perch segment.

13. Glue the middle perch segment between the feet where indicated by the dashed lines on 7–3. Have the perch-support hole face in the direction of the arrow on 7–3.

14. Glue the outer perch segments to the outside of the feet where indicated by the dashed lines on 7–3.

15. Paint the lower legs and feet pale blue-grey. Moisten the sponge with water and squeeze almost dry. Dab the sponge into charcoal grey and tamp

onto paper towelling to remove the excess. Dab over the lower legs and feet, making an irregular pattern. Paint the claws charcoal grey. Referring to the Materials list for the colors, paint the rest of the body as shown on 7–1 to 7–3 and the color photograph. Extend the colors onto the edge surfaces. (Don't paint into the tinted gluing areas or the notch at the back of the body.)

16. Paint the lower half of the eyes white. Paint a thin pale blue-grey ring around the center of the white area. Paint the irises pale blue-grey and the pupils black.

17. Glue the right red tail feather (7–4) (top of assembly) onto the left red tail feather. Align their straight ends (indicated by the diamond on the pattern), and space the tips of their tails 2½″ apart.

18. On the underside of the assembly made in Step 17, measure 2″ down from the straight end for the gluing area. Paint both sides of the red tail feathers. (Don't paint into the gluing area.)

19. On one side of the blue tail feather (7–5), measure 2″ down from the straight end (indicated by the diamond on the pattern) for the gluing area and ½″ down from the straight end on the other side. Paint the blue tail feather. (Don't paint into the gluing areas.)

20. With the 2″ gluing areas facing, glue the red tail feather assembly to the blue tail feather. Have the straight ends aligned and centered on each other.

21. Glue the completed tail feather assembly to the notch at the back of the body where indicated by the arrows on 7–1 (see color photo).

22. To create the angle on the underside of each bottom wing (7–6), whittle a flat surface from the dashed line to the star so that the thickness at the star is ³⁄₁₆″.

23. Paint both sides of the wings as shown on 7–6, 7–7, and 7–8. Extend the colors in a curve onto the edge surfaces, as shown in 7–10. (Don't paint into the gluing areas or wing angles.)

24. With their upper edges aligned, as shown in the color photograph, glue the bottom, middle, and top wings together. See 7–10 for a front view of the completed wings.

25. Glue the wing angles to the body where indicated by the large dashed lines on 7–1. At the

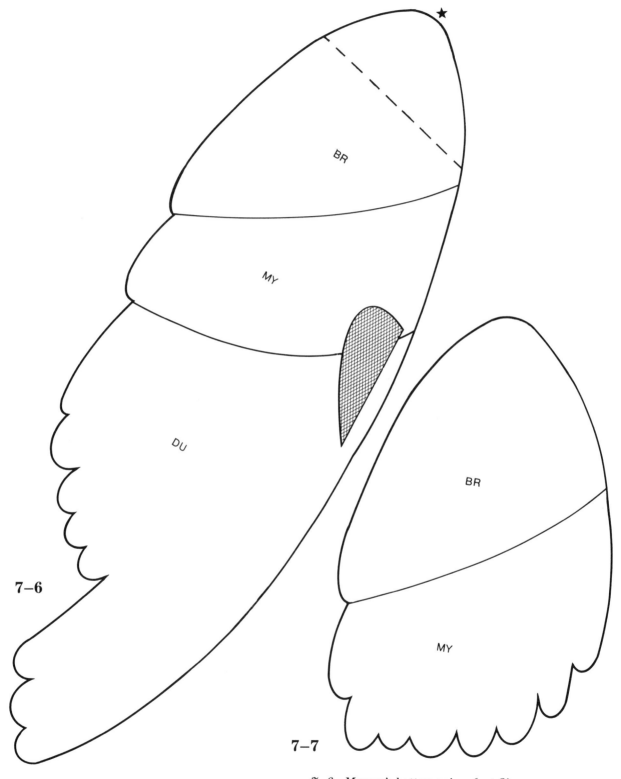

7–6. *Macaw's bottom wing (cut 2).*
7–7. *Macaw's middle wing (cut 2).*

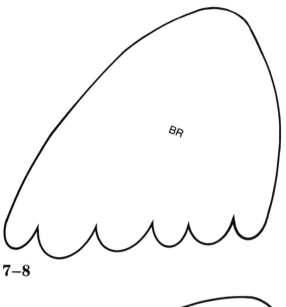

7–8

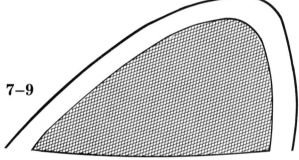

7–9

7–10. Front of the macaw.

7–8. Macaw's top wing (cut 2).
7–9. Pattern for the gluing areas of the bottom, middle, and top wings.

same time, adhere the gluing areas on the underside of the bottom wings (7–6) to the top of the legs.

26. Paint the perch with alternating horizontal strokes of black and dark red-brown. Lightly blend the strokes together to simulate bark. (Don't paint into the perch-support hole.)

27. Apply the high-gloss finish.

28. Use tacky glue to adhere the feather fluffs to the macaw. Have the shaft end of the feathers pointed up in all cases. Refer to 7–10 and the color photograph.

29. Glue the 7″-long yellow feather fluff to the top

of the blue tail feather, tucking its shaft end under the angle of the red tail feathers.

30. Glue the two blue feather fluffs to the macaw's back just above the red tail feathers. Have their shaft ends angled up and touching at the center of the edge surface.

31. On the front and back edge surfaces of the macaw's body, glue a red feather fluff where the red and yellow paint meet, and a yellow feather fluff where the yellow and blue paint meet.

32. Glue the shaft ends of five red feather fluffs between the top and middle wings, spacing them evenly across. Glue the shaft ends of five yellow feather fluffs between the middle and bottom wings.

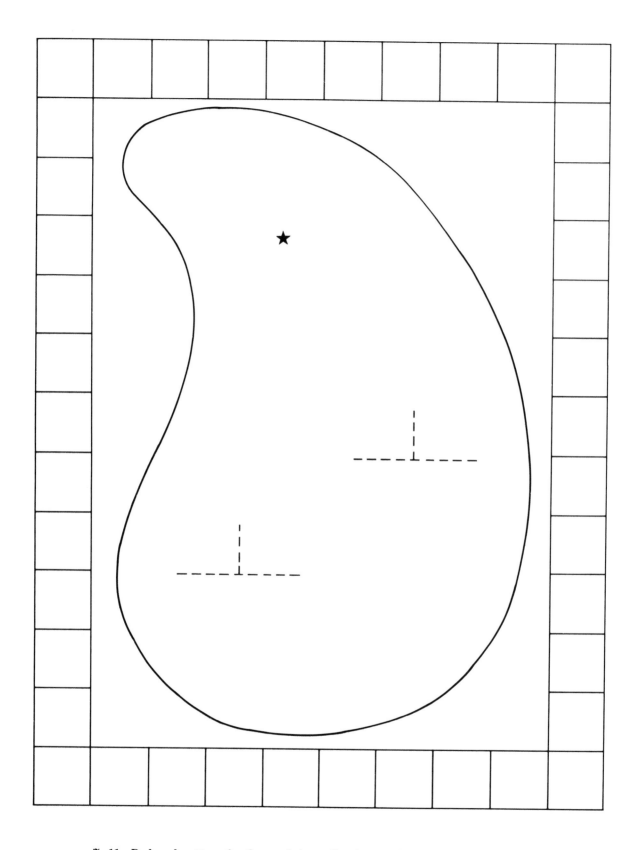

7–11. *Reduced pattern for the perch base. One box = 1″ × 1″. Enlarge and cut 1.*

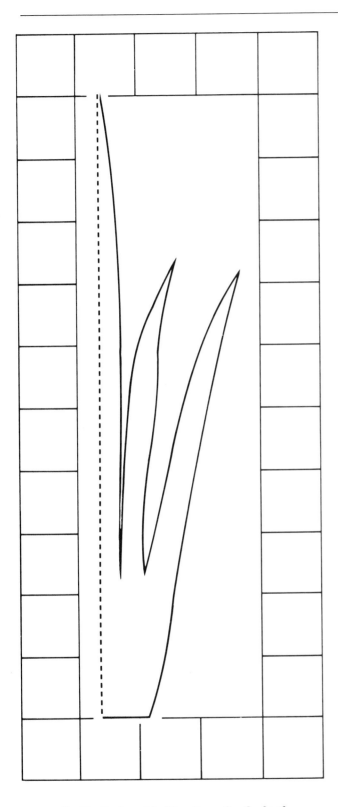

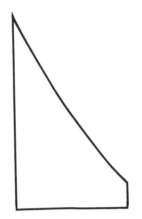

7–13. Bush support (cut 2).

Perch

1. Cut one base (7–11) from 1 × 10 pine.

2. Cut two bushes (7–12) and two bush supports (7–13) from ¼ × 5¼ lattice.

3. Using the ⅜″ bit, drill a ⅝″-deep hole into the base (7–11), where indicated by the star, for the perch support.

4. With the bottom edges even, glue one bush support (7–13) on its long side at a right angle to the center back of each bush (7–12).

5. Position the bushes on the base where indicated by the dashed lines. Draw the outline of the base of each bush on the base with a pencil.

6. Paint the base very dark grey-green. (Don't paint into the perch support hole or within the bush base outlines.) Moisten a sponge with water and squeeze almost dry. Dab the sponge into the very dark grey-green, and tamp onto paper towelling to remove the excess. Then dab into light yellow-green, and tamp onto towelling to remove the excess. Dab over the top and sides of the base, making an irregular pattern, as shown in the color photograph.

7. Paint the bushes light yellow-green. (Don't paint the underside of the bushes.) Glue the bushes to the base.

7–12. Reduced half-pattern for the bush. One box = 1″ × 1″. Enlarge and cut 2.

8. Use the 18″ length of ⅜″ dowelling for the perch support. Whittle ⅜″ at one end (the top of the support) to a ¼″-diameter peg that fits snugly into the hole in the perch segment between the macaw's feet.

9. Paint the perch support with alternating vertical strokes of black and dark red-brown. Lightly blend the strokes together to simulate bark. (Don't paint the peg or ⅝″ of the bottom.)

10. Glue the unpainted bottom of the perch support into the hole in the base.

11. Apply the high-gloss finish to the base, bushes, and perch support.

12. To assemble, insert the peg end of the perch support into the hole in the middle perch segment between the macaw's feet.

8. Toucan

There are 37 species of these vividly colored large-billed birds that are found from the middle of Central America to southwestern South America. They nest in tree cavities and are fruit eaters. Although a toucan's bill looks heavy and cumbersome, it is actually very light because it is only a shell of horny tissue with a hollow interior.

Toucan*

1. Cut one body (8–1) from 1 × 10 pine. Saw through the beak along the dashed line.

2. Cut two each of the top, middle, and bottom wings (8–2) from ¼ × 5¼ lattice. The pattern shows the orientation of the left wing; the right wing is a mirror image.

3. Cut one top (8–3), one middle (8–4), and one bottom (8–5) tail feather from ¼ × 5¼ lattice.

4. Using the ⁷⁄₃₂″ bit, drill ⁵⁄₁₆-deep axle peg holes, where indicated by the stars on 8–1, on both sides of the body (8–1).

5. Glue the top, middle, and bottom wings together (8–2). Align the edges as shown on the pattern. Using the ⁷⁄₃₂″ bit, drill an axle peg hole, where indicated by the star on 8–2, through each wing assembly.

6. Using the ¼″ bit, drill a ½″-deep hole, where indicated by the arrow on 8–1, into the bottom edge of the feet for the perch support.

---

*Refer to the General Directions for the techniques needed to complete this project.

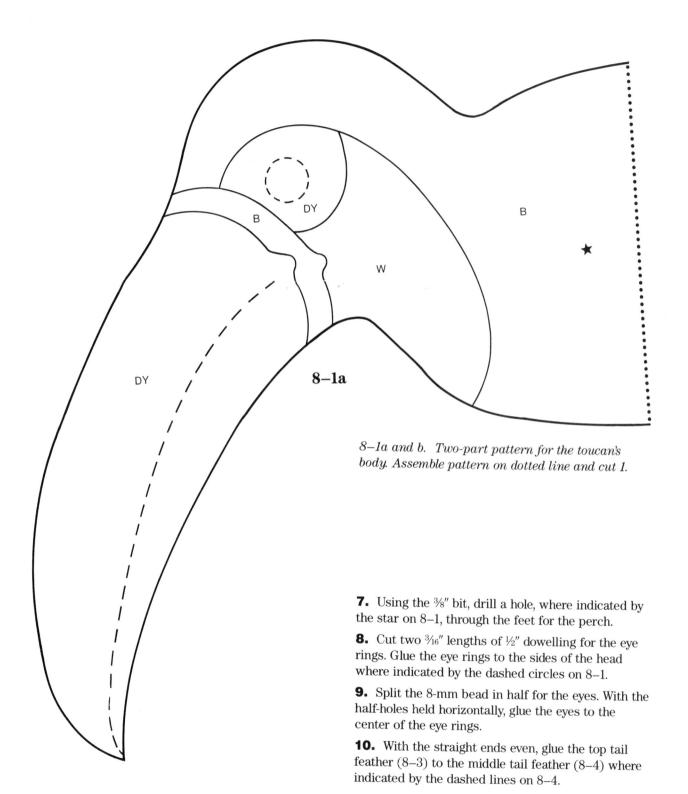

B

DY

B

W

DY

★

8–1a

8–1a and b. Two-part pattern for the toucan's body. Assemble pattern on dotted line and cut 1.

7. Using the ⅜″ bit, drill a hole, where indicated by the star on 8–1, through the feet for the perch.

8. Cut two ³⁄₁₆″ lengths of ½″ dowelling for the eye rings. Glue the eye rings to the sides of the head where indicated by the dashed circles on 8–1.

9. Split the 8-mm bead in half for the eyes. With the half-holes held horizontally, glue the eyes to the center of the eye rings.

10. With the straight ends even, glue the top tail feather (8–3) to the middle tail feather (8–4) where indicated by the dashed lines on 8–4.

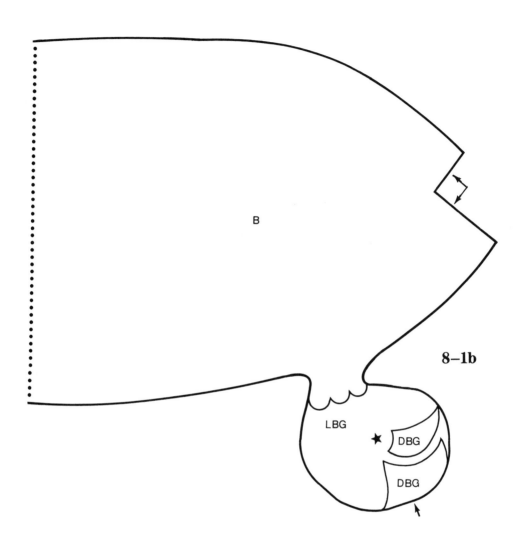

11. Glue the straight ends of the tail–feather assembly to the notch at the back of the body where indicated by the arrows on 8–1 and as shown in 8–6.

12. Glue the bottom tail feather (8–5) under the middle tail feather (8–4). Butt its straight end to the back edge of the body, and center it from side to side on the straight end of the middle tail feather. See 8–6 for the completed tail.

13. Referring to the Materials list for the colors, paint the toucan as shown on 8–1 to 8–6 and in the color photograph. (Don't paint into the holes for the axle pegs, the perch support, or the perch.) Extend the colors onto the edge surfaces.

14. Paint the eye rings medium-blue metallic and the eyes black. Highlight the right eye with a small white crescent at 5 o'clock and the left eye at 7 o'clock. Paint the axle peg caps black.

15. Apply the high-gloss finish to all parts.

16. To attach each wing, apply a small amount of glue into a peg hole in the shoulder of the body (8–1). Insert an axle peg through the peg hole in the corresponding wing assembly and then into the

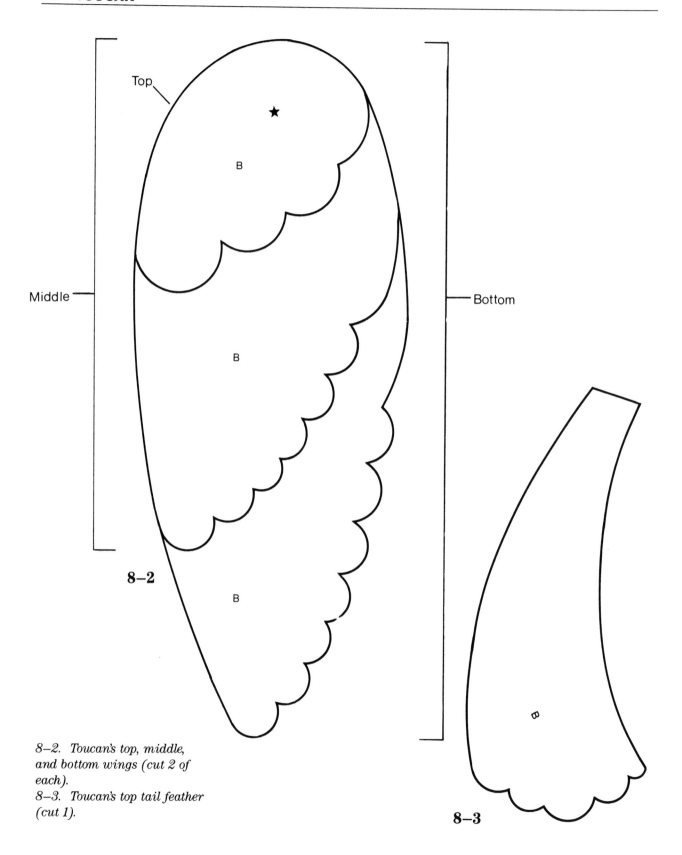

Top

Middle

Bottom

B

B

B

B

8–2

8–2. Toucan's top, middle, and bottom wings (cut 2 of each).
8–3. Toucan's top tail feather (cut 1).

8–3

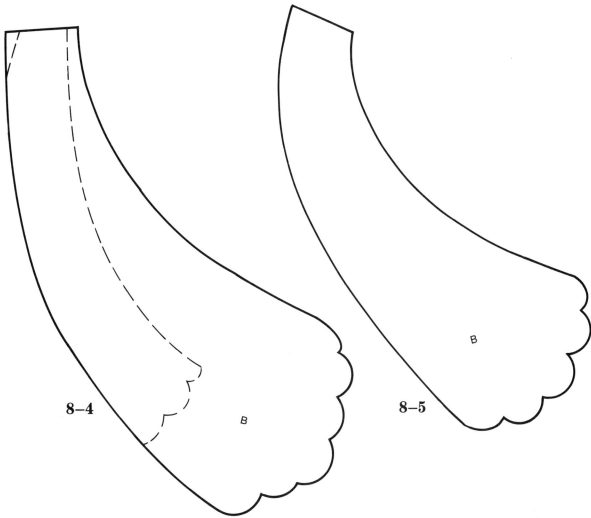

8–4. *Toucan's middle tail feather (cut 1).*
8–5. *Toucan's bottom tail feather (cut 1).*

glued peg hole in the body. The wings should be able
to move up and down and hold a pose.

Perch

1. Cut one base (8–7) from 1 × 10 pine.

2. Cut three bushes (8–8) and three bush supports
(8–9) from ¼ × 5¼ lattice.

3. Using the $^7/_{16}$″ bit, drill a $^5/_8$″-deep hole, where
indicated by the star, into the base (8–7), for the
perch support.

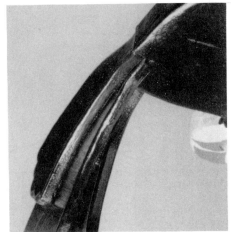

8–6. *Toucan's tail-feather assembly (back view).*

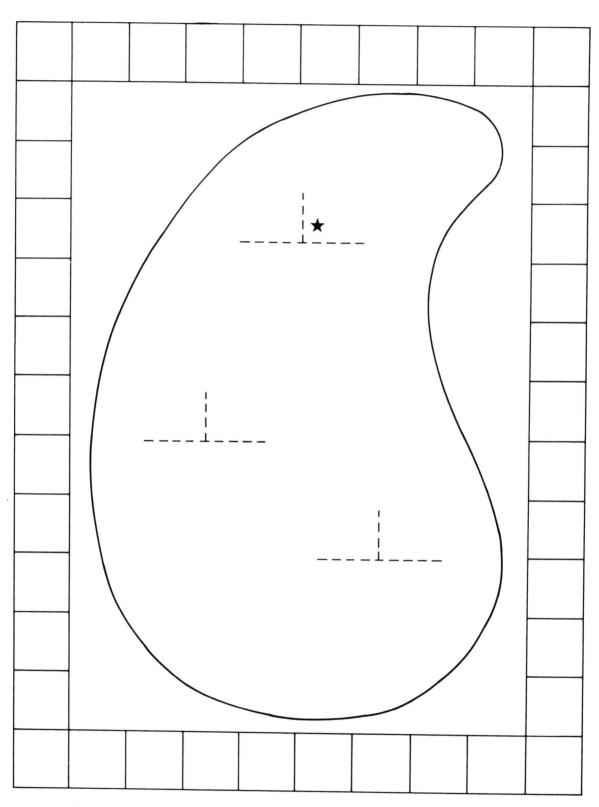

8–7. *Reduced pattern for the perch base. One box = 1″ × 1″. Enlarge and cut 1.*

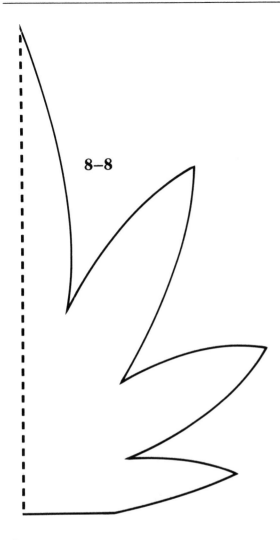

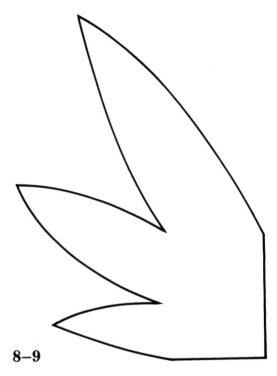

8–8. *Half-pattern for the bush (cut 3).*
8–9. *Bush support (cut 3).*

4. With the bottom edges even, glue one bush support (8–9) at right angles to the center back of each bush (8–8).

5. Position the bushes on the base where indicated by the dashed lines on 8–7. With a pencil, draw the outline of the bottom of each bush and support on 8–7.

6. Paint the base (8–7) very dark grey-green. (Don't paint into the perch support hole or within the bush outlines.) Moisten the sponge with water and squeeze it almost dry. Dab the sponge into the very dark grey-green, and tamp it onto paper towelling to remove the excess. Then dab it into light yellow-green, and tamp it onto towelling to remove the excess. Dab it over the top and sides of the base, making an irregular pattern, as shown in the color photograph.

7. Paint the bushes light yellow-green. (Don't paint the undersides of the bushes.) Glue the bushes to the base.

8. Use the 10″ length of 7/16″ dowelling for the perch support. Whittle ½″ of one end (the top of the support) to a ¼″-diameter peg that fits snugly into the hole in the toucan's feet.

9. Paint the perch support with alternating vertical strokes of black and dark red-brown. Lightly blend the strokes together to simulate bark. (Don't paint the peg or 5/8″ of the bottom of the support.)

10. Glue the unpainted bottom of the perch support into the hole in the base (8–7).

11. Apply the high-gloss finish to the base, bushes, and perch support.

12. To assemble, insert the peg end of the perch support into the hole in the bottom of the toucan's feet. Insert the twigs into the perch holes in the sides of the feet. Whittle the twig ends to fit if necessary.

9. Spider Monkeys

Spider monkeys are forest dwellers and can be found from Mexico to Brazil. They live in bands, high in the treetops, and rarely ever descend to the ground. There are 4 species of spider monkey and all are agile and quick. They swing through the branches, using their hands and long, prehensile tails, and sometimes leap from tree to tree. Spider monkeys feed on fruits, nuts, flowers, and buds, and grow 14 to 26 inches long.

Father Monkey*

1. Cut one body (9–1) and one head (9–2) from 1 × 6 pine.

2. Cut two legs (9–3), two ears (9–4), one right arm (9–5), one left arm (9–6), and one tail (9–7) from ¼ × 5¼ lattice.

3. Using the ¹⁵⁄₆₄″ bit, drill a ¾″-deep neck hole and a ⁵⁄₁₆″-deep tail hole where indicated by the arrows on the body (9–1). Drill a ¾″-deep neck hole where indicated by the arrow on the head (9–2).

---

*Refer to the General Directions for the techniques needed to complete this project.

MATERIALS

- 50″ length of ¼ × 5¼ clear pine lattice
- 12″ length of 1 × 6 clear pine
- 7″ length of ¼″ dowelling
- Twelve 1¼″-long × ¼″-diameter wooden axle pegs
- Drill bits: ⁷⁄₃₂″ and ¹⁵⁄₆₄″
- Small amounts of light brown and white fake furs
- Acrylic paints: light red-brown, light apricot, light pink, black, and white
- High-gloss finish

4. Using the ⁷⁄₃₂″ bit, drill four ¼″-deep axle peg holes, where indicated by the stars, on both sides of the body (9–1). Then drill axle peg holes, where indicated by the stars, through the legs (9–3) and the arms (9–5 and 9–6).

5. Cut a 1½″ length of ¼″ dowelling for the neck peg.

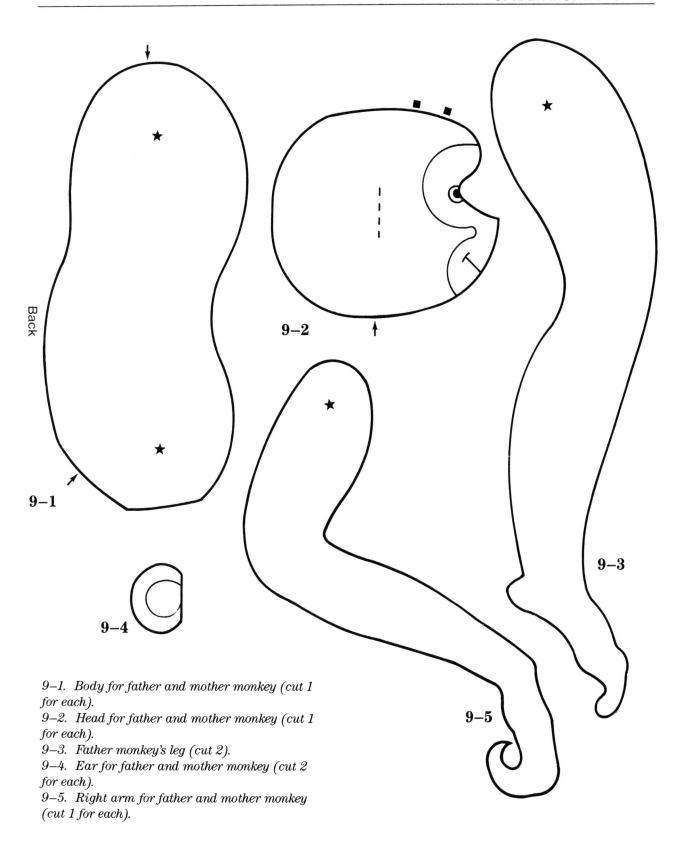

Back

9–1

9–2

9–3

9–4

9–5

9–1. *Body for father and mother monkey (cut 1 for each).*

9–2. *Head for father and mother monkey (cut 1 for each).*

9–3. *Father monkey's leg (cut 2).*

9–4. *Ear for father and mother monkey (cut 2 for each).*

9–5. *Right arm for father and mother monkey (cut 1 for each).*

6. Apply glue to the neck peg and insert it into the neck hole in the head (9–2).

7. Glue the ears (9–4) to the sides of the head where indicated by the dashed lines.

8. Round the edges of the peg end of the tail by whittling so that it will fit snugly into the tail hole in the body. Apply glue to the tail peg and insert it into the tail hole.

9. Trim ½″ from the ends of the axle pegs so that each measures ¾″ from the top of the cap to the bottom of the peg.

10. Paint the body, tail, arms, legs, and axle peg caps light red-brown. (Don't paint the neck peg or into the neck and axle peg holes.)

11. As shown in 9–8 and in the color photo, paint the head and the ears light red-brown. Paint the face light apricot and the inner ears light pink. Outline the inner ears with black. Paint the eyes white and the nose light red-brown. Use black to paint the mouth, nostrils, pupils, and top eyelids.

12. Apply the high-gloss finish to all parts.

13. To attach each arm and leg, apply a small amount of glue in the corresponding peg hole in the body. Insert an axle peg through the peg hole in the corresponding limb and then into the glued peg hole in the body. The arms and legs should be able to move up and down and hold a pose.

14. For the head fur, cut a ¼″ × ⅝″ rectangle of light brown fake fur. Use tacky glue to adhere the fur between the squares on the head (9–2).

15. For the neck fur, cut a ⁷⁄₁₆″ × 3″ rectangle of light brown fake fur. Overlap the ends ⅛″ to form a ring and secure with tacky glue.

16. To attach the head, insert the neck peg into the fur ring and then into the neck hole in the top of the body (do not glue). The head should be able to move from right to left.

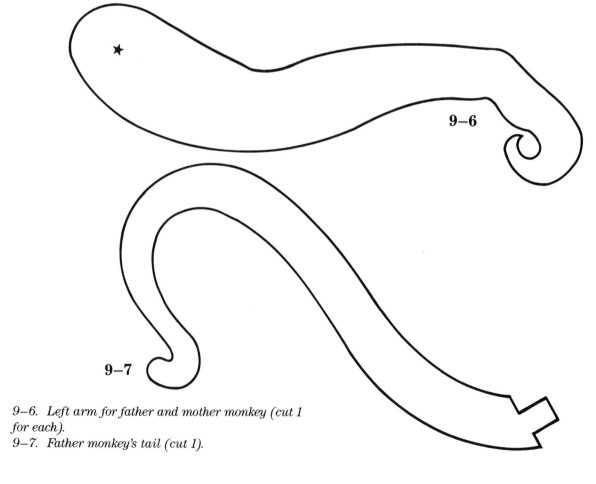

9–6. Left arm for father and mother monkey (cut 1 for each).
9–7. Father monkey's tail (cut 1).

9–8. Parent and baby monkeys' faces.

Mother Monkey

1. Cut one body (9–1) and one head (9–2) from 1 × 6 pine.

2. Cut two legs (9–9), two ears (9–4), one right arm (9–5), one left arm (9–6), and one tail (9–10) from ¼ × 5¼ lattice.

3. Repeat Steps 3 to 16 of the father monkey instructions.

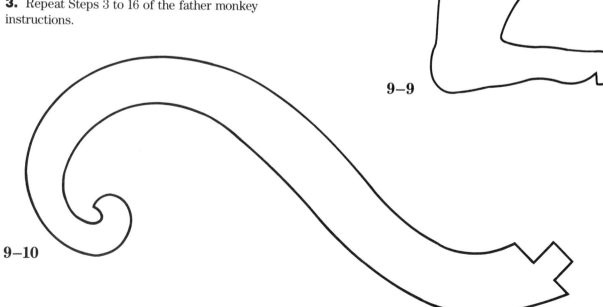

9–9

9–10

9–9. *Mother monkey's leg (cut 2).*
9–10. *Mother monkey's tail (cut 1).*

Baby Monkey

1. Cut one body (9–11) and one head (9–12) from 1 × 6 pine.

2. Cut two legs (9–13), two ears (9–14), one right arm (9–15), one left arm (9–16), and one tail (9–17) from ¼ × 5¼ lattice.

3. Repeat Steps 3 to 13 of the father monkey instructions.

4. For the head fur, cut a ¼″ × ⅝″ rectangle of light brown fake fur. Use tacky glue to adhere the fur between the squares on the head (9–12).

5. For the neck fur, cut a ⁷⁄₁₆″ × 2½″ rectangle of white fake fur. Overlap the ends ⅛″ to form a ring and secure with tacky glue.

6. Repeat Step 16 of the father monkey instructions.

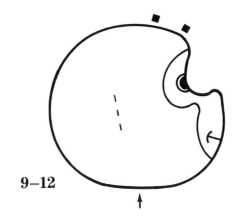

9–12

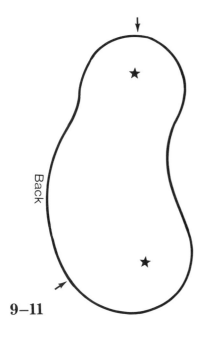

9–11

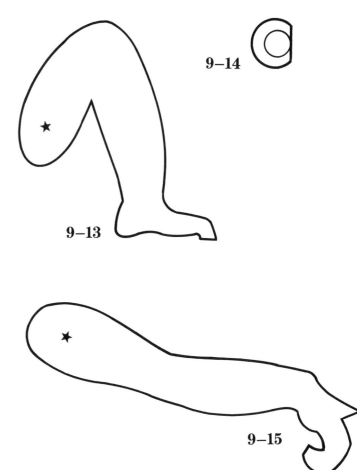

9–14

9–13

9–15

9–11. *Baby monkey's body (cut 1).*
9–12. *Baby monkey's head (cut 1).*
9–13. *Baby monkey's leg (cut 2).*
9–14. *Baby monkey's ear (cut 2).*
9–15. *Baby monkey's right arm (cut 1).*

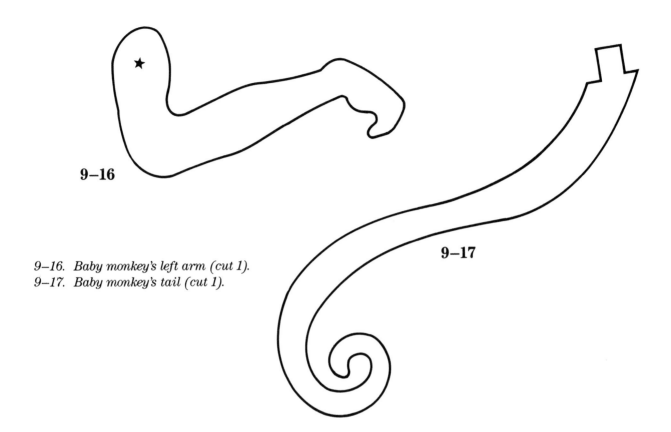

9-16

9-17

9-16. *Baby monkey's left arm (cut 1).*
9-17. *Baby monkey's tail (cut 1).*

10. Lion Pull Toy

Lions inhabit the grassy plains and open woodlands of west, east, and southern Africa. Hunting in groups, they pursue herds of antelope, wildebeest, and zebra. Lions are the only cats that live in permanent groups. Called prides, these groups may contain up to 25 individuals, including as many as 6 adult males. Lions measure 7 to 8 feet long, including the tail, and can weigh up to 420 pounds (191 kg).

MATERIALS

- 36″ length of ¼ × 5¼ clear pine lattice
- 20″ length of ½ × 5½ clear pine lattice
- 13″ length of 1 × 12 clear pine
- Four 1⅝″-long × ⅜″-diameter wooden axle pegs
- One 1½″-diameter wooden wheel
- Four 2½″-diameter wooden wheels
- One white 25-mm large-hole round wood bead

- Drill bits: No. 61 (wire gauge), ¹⁄₁₆″, ⅛″, ⁵⁄₃₂″, and ⁵⁄₁₆″

- Four #6 × 1½″ flat-head wood screws
- Four #19 × ½″ wire brads
- Two #18 × 1¼″ wire brads
- Four ¼″ flat washers

- 9″ length of paper cord
- Scrap of black synthetic suede
- 36″ length of leather boot lace

- Acrylic paint: medium gold, ochre, dark brown, black, white, medium yellow-green, and light yellow-green
- Satin finish

Lion*

1. Cut one body (10–1) from 1 × 12 pine.

2. Cut two front legs (10–2) and two back legs (10–3) from ½ × 5½ lattice.

3. Cut one center mane (10–4), four side manes (10–5), two top manes (10–6), one front bang (10–7), two ears (10–8), one nose (10–9), and one tail tip (10–10) from ¼ × 5¼ lattice. The side-mane pattern (10–5) shows the orientation for the right front and left back side manes; the left front and right back side manes are mirror images. (See Step 8.) The ear pattern (10–8) shows the details of the right ear; the left ear is a mirror image of 10–8.

---

*Refer to the General Directions for the techniques needed to complete this project.

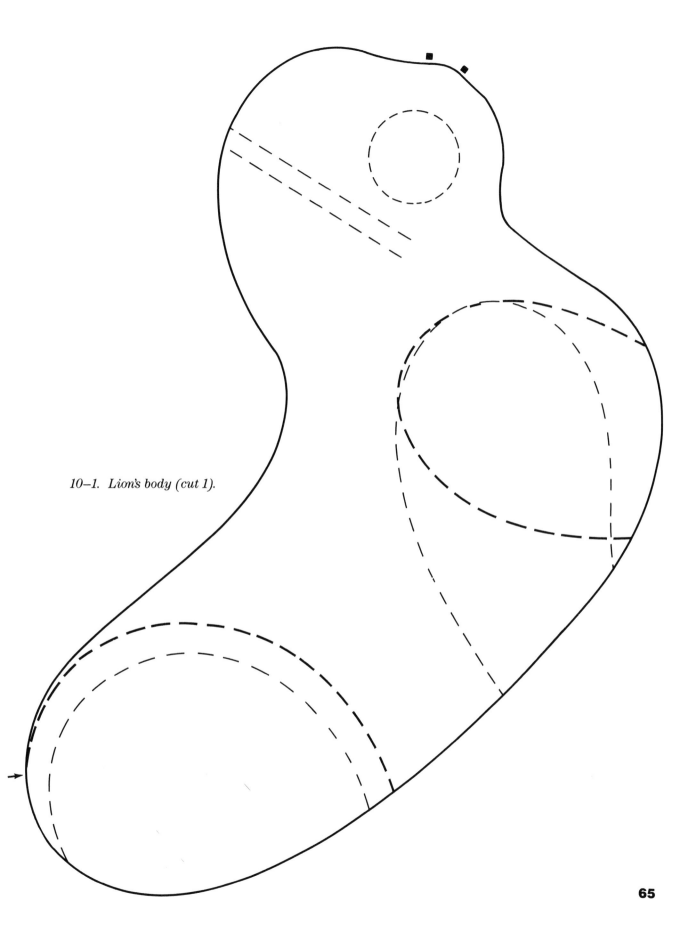

10–1. Lion's body (cut 1).

65

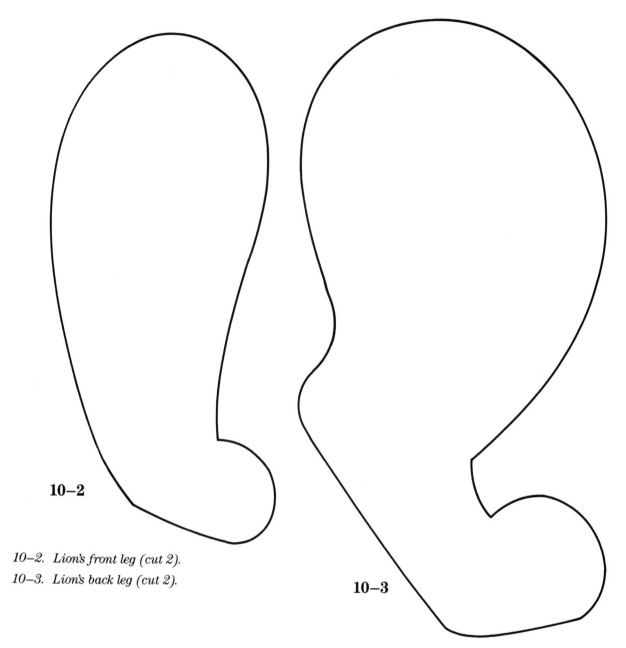

10–2

10–2. Lion's front leg (cut 2).
10–3. Lion's back leg (cut 2).

10–3

4. Using the ⁵⁄₃₂″ bit, drill a ½″-deep tail hole where indicated by the arrow on the body (10–1) and a ¼″-deep tail hole where indicated by the arrow on the tail tip (10–10).

5. Glue the right front and back legs to the right side of the body where indicated by the light dashed lines on 10–1 and the left front and back legs to the left side where indicated by the heavy dashed lines. Make sure that the feet rest flat on the work surface.

6. Split the 25-mm bead in half for the cheeks. Sand the cut surfaces to eliminate the half-holes. Glue the cheeks to the sides of the head where indicated by the dashed circles on 10–1.

7. Glue the center mane (10–4) to the head where indicated by the dashed lines on 10–1.

8. Whittle a 45° angle from the dashed line to the straight edge of each side mane (10–5). The pattern shows the dashed line for the right front and left

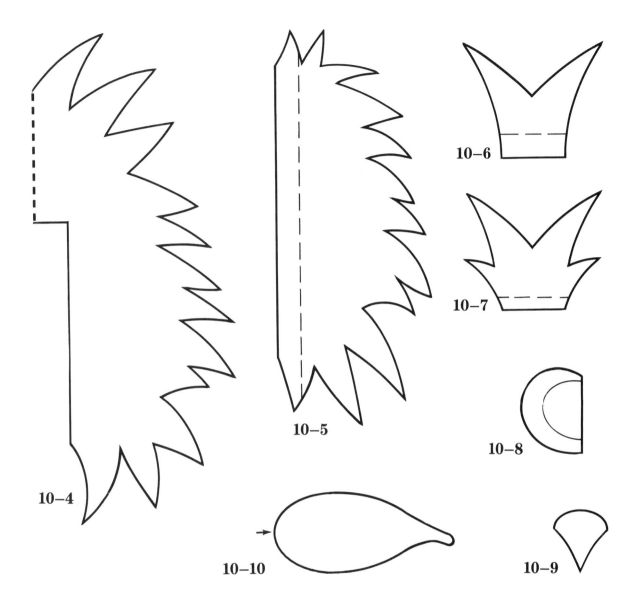

10–6

10–7

10–5

10–8

10–4

10–10

10–9

10–4. *Half-pattern for the lion's center mane (cut 1).*
10–5. *Lion's side mane (cut 4).*
10–6. *Lion's top mane (cut 2).*
10–7. *Lion's front bang (cut 1).*
10–8. *Lion's ear (cut 2).*
10–9. *Lion's nose (cut 1).*
10–10. *Lion's tail tip (cut 1).*

back manes. Flop the pattern and the remaining two manes over, and transfer the dashed line to the left front and right back manes.

9. Apply glue to the angles of the side manes, and position them on the head as shown in 10–11 and 10–12. Adhere the angles to the center mane, have the straight edges flush against the head, and center the side manes from top to bottom on the center mane.

10. Whittle the edge of each top mane (10–6) to a 45° angle, working from the dashed line to the straight edge.

11. Glue the angle of one top mane to the back of the head with its straight edge flush against the center mane, as shown in 10–11. Glue the angle of the other top mane to the front of the head with its straight edge flush against the center mane, as shown in 10–12.

12. Whittle the edge of the front bang (10–7) to a 22° angle, working from the dashed line to the straight edge.

13. Glue the front bang to the top of the head with the angle flush against the front mane, as shown in 10–12.

14. On both sides of each ear (10–8), mark a line ¼″ from and parallel with the straight edge. Working from the marked lines towards the straight edges, whittle both sides of the ear to identical angles.

15. Whittle the underside of the nose (10–9) as needed to fit the contour of the face. Glue the nose to the front of the head where indicated by the squares on 10–1.

16. Use the 9″ length of paper cord for the tail. Use tacky glue to adhere one end into the hole in the tail tip (10–10) and the opposite end into the tail hole in the body.

17. Paint the body, head, legs, tail, and ears medium gold. Use ochre to paint the mane and tail tip. Using dark brown, paint the nose and inner ears.

18. Use black to paint the face details shown in 10–12. Use white to highlight both eyes at 3 o'clock.

19. Use tacky glue to adhere the ears between the front and center manes, as shown in 10–12, aligning the top of the ears with the top of the head.

20. Cut six ¹⁄₁₆″ × ¹⁵⁄₁₆″ strips of black synthetic suede for the whiskers. Use tacky glue to adhere them below the nose, as shown in 10–12.

Platform

1. Cut a 5⅜″ × 13″ rectangle from 1 × 12 pine for the platform.

2. Cut three bushes (10–13) from ¼ × 5¼ lattice.

3. On the edge surface of both long sides of the

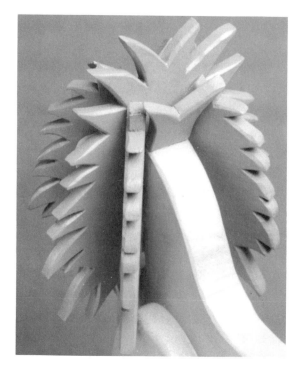

10–11. Back view of the lion's mane.

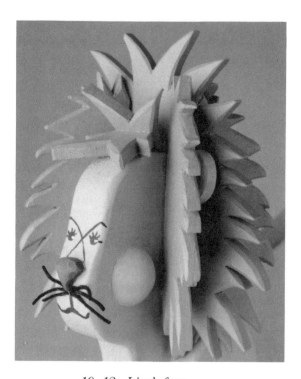

10–12. Lion's face.

platform, mark for two axle-peg holes, 2″ from the front and back edges (from the short sides) and centered from top to bottom. Using the ⁵⁄₁₆″ bit, drill ¾″-deep holes.

4. On the center of the edge surface of one short side, mark for the pull hole. (This is now the front of the platform.) Using the ⅛″ bit, drill a 1″-deep hole.

5. Place the platform on the work surface with the back facing you. Mark the position of two pilot holes for the bush that will be secured to the top of the platform. One hole is 3¾″ from the back edge and ⅝″ in from the left edge. One hole is 4¾″ from the back edge and ⅝″ in from the left edge. Using the No. 61 bit, drill pilot holes through the platform.

6. Place the platform on the work surface with the back facing you. Referring to the photograph at the beginning of the project, stand the lion on the platform. Position the tip of his left paw 1½″ from the front of the platform, and center him from side to side. Use a pencil to trace the outline of each paw. Mark the center of each outline for a pilot hole. Using the ¹⁄₁₆″ bit, drill pilot holes through the platform.

7. Insert the screws from the underside of the platform so that their tips extend slightly above the top surface. Place the lion on the platform, centering his paws over the screw tips, and press slightly to make indentions in the bottom of the paws. Remove the screws from the platform.

8. Using the ¹⁄₁₆″ bit, drill ¾″-deep pilot holes into the bottom of each paw.

9. Apply glue to the bottom edge of one bush, and center it over the pilot holes in the platform. Secure it to the platform using two #18 × 1¼″ brads hammered from the underside.

10. As shown in the photograph at the beginning of the project, center the two remaining bushes between the axle peg holes on either side of the platform and have the bushes' bottom edges even with the bottom of the platform. Apply glue and secure them with two #19 × ½″ brads.

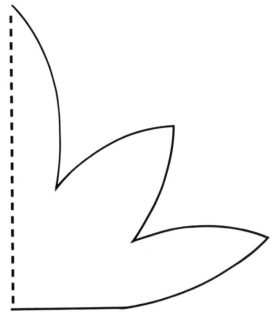

10–13. Half-pattern for bush (cut 3).

11. Paint the bushes medium yellow-green. Use light yellow-green to paint the platform. Use the ochre to paint the 1½″-diameter wheel used for the pull knob.

12. Secure the lion to the platform with the screws.

13. Apply the satin finish to the entire assembly, pull knob, 2½″-diameter wheels, and axle peg caps.

14. To attach each wheel, apply a small amount of glue into an axle peg hole in the platform. Insert an axle peg through the hole in a wheel, through a washer, and then into the glued axle peg hole in the platform. The wheels should be able to spin freely.

15. Use tacky glue to adhere one end of the boot lace into the pull hole in the platform. Knot the lacing 3″ from the free end. Draw the free end through the hole in the pull knob. Knot the free end close to the knob, and trim the end close to the knot.

11. Giraffe Pull Toy

- 14″ length of ¼ × 5¼ clear pine lattice
- 26″ length of ½ × 5½ clear pine lattice
- 18″ length of 1 × 12 clear pine

- Four 1¼″-long × ¼″-diameter wooden axle pegs
- Four 1⅝″-long × ⅜″-diameter wooden axle pegs
- One 1½″-diameter wooden wheel
- Four 2½″-diameter wooden wheels
- Two white 10-mm regular-hole round wood beads
- One round toothpick

- Drill bits: ¹⁄₁₆″, ³⁄₁₆″, and ⁵⁄₁₆″

- Four #6 × 1½″ flat-head wood screws
- Four ¼″ flat washers

- Two 2″ × 2″ squares of stencil blank
- Masking tape
- 1″ × 1″ cellulose sponge
- 40″-long brown flat-woven boot lace
- 6 yards of light brown three-ply Persian yarn

- Acrylic paint: light lemon yellow, dark brown, white, black, medium taupe, dark grey, and medium yellow-green
- Satin finish

Giraffes live on the grasslands of central, eastern, and southern Africa. At maturity, males weigh up to 2,800 pounds (1273 kg) and are nearly 19 feet in height, which makes them the tallest animals on earth. Baby giraffes stand 6 feet tall at birth and weigh about 150 pounds (68 kg)! Giraffes have good eyesight and can run 35 miles (56 km) per hour when in danger. Their diet consists of twigs, bark, and leaves, especially those of the acacia tree.

Male Giraffe*

1. Cut one body (11–1) from 1 × 12 pine.

2. Cut two front legs (11–2) and two back legs (11–3) from ½ × 5½ lattice. Cut across the hooves for the right front and left back legs along the bottom solid lines. Cut across the hooves for the left front and the right back legs along the dashed lines.

3. Cut two ears (11–4) from ¼ × 5¼ lattice. The pattern shows the orientation of the right ear; the left ear is a mirror image.

---

*Refer to the General Directions for the techniques needed to complete this project.

4. Using the ¹⁄₁₆″ bit, drill a ¼″-deep tail hole where indicated by the arrow on the body (11–1).

5. On the front surface of the head, where indicated by the arrow on 11–1, mark ³⁄₁₆″ in from both side edges. Using the ¼″ bit, drill ¼″-deep horn holes. Angle the bit for the right horn hole towards the bottom of the left cheek and for the left horn hole towards the bottom of the right cheek. (See 11–5 for the completed head.)

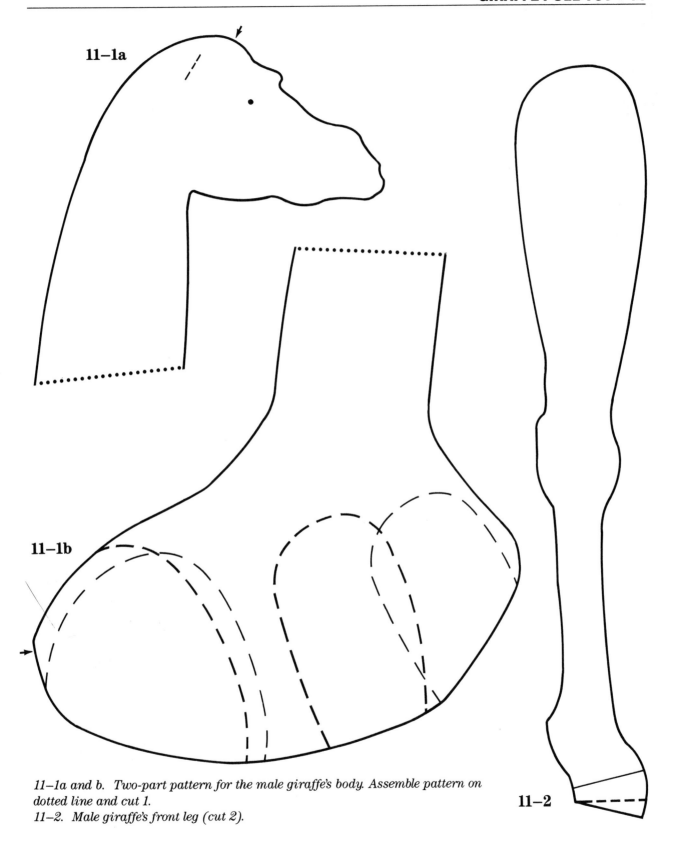

11–1a

11–1b

11–2

11–1a and b. Two-part pattern for the male giraffe's body. Assemble pattern on dotted line and cut 1.
11–2. Male giraffe's front leg (cut 2).

11–3

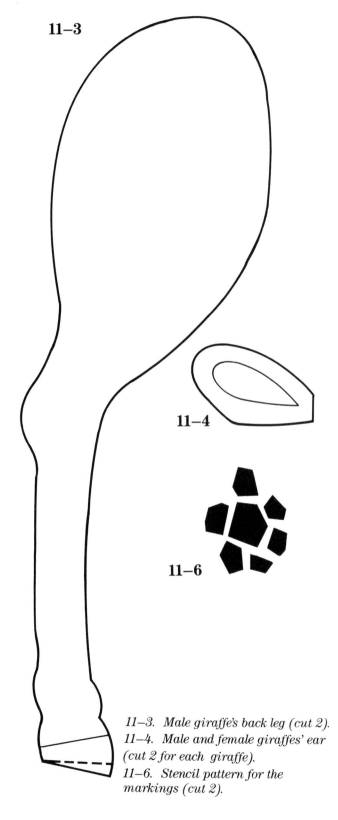

11–4

11–6

11–3. *Male giraffe's back leg (cut 2).*
11–4. *Male and female giraffes' ear (cut 2 for each giraffe).*
11–6. *Stencil pattern for the markings (cut 2).*

6. Glue the right front and back legs to the right side of the body where indicated by the light dashed lines on 11–1 and the left front and back legs to the left side where indicated by the heavy dashed lines. Make sure that the hooves rest flat on the work surface.

7. Split a 10-mm bead in half for the eyes. With the half-holes held parallel with the brow ridge, glue the eyes to both sides of head where indicated by the dots on 11–1. Fill the half-holes with paste wood filler, allow to dry, and sand smooth.

8. Glue one 1¼"-long × ¼"-diameter axle peg into each horn hole.

9. Glue the ears to the sides of the head where indicated by the dashed lines on the head (11–1).

10. Paint the body and horns light lemon-yellow. (Don't paint into the tail hole.) Use dark brown to paint the inner ears and nostrils.

11. Referring to 11–5, paint the lower half of the eyes white with black pupils. For the eyelids, paint the upper half of the eyes light lemon-yellow. Use medium taupe to paint a dotted line along the edge of the eyelids.

11–5. *Male giraffe's face.*

12. Paint the hooves dark grey. (Don't paint the underside of the hooves.) Use black to paint a $\frac{1}{16}''$-wide line down the center front of each hoof.

13. Transfer the stencil pattern (11–6) onto the center of both stencil blanks. Cut out the stencil using a craft knife. Position one stencil on the giraffe and secure with masking tape. Refer to the color photograph for a suggested arrangement of the markings. Moisten the sponge with water and squeeze almost dry. Dab the sponge into dark brown paint, and tamp onto paper towelling to remove excess paint; then dab the sponge evenly over the stencil. Remove the tape and lift off the stencil. Allow the paint to dry before stencilling the next pattern. Vary the angle of the stencil, as shown in the photograph. Trim the other stencil as needed so that it can fit into tight spaces.

Female Giraffe

1. Cut one body (11–7) from 1×12 pine. (The body is the solid line on the pattern.)

2. Cut one head (11–8) and one neck (11–9) from $\frac{1}{2} \times 5\frac{1}{2}$ lattice.

3. Cut one right front leg (11–10), one left front leg (11–11), and two back legs (11–12) from $\frac{1}{2} \times 5\frac{1}{2}$ lattice.

4. Repeat Steps 3 and 4 of the male giraffe.

5. On the front surface of the head, where indicated by the arrow on 11–8, mark $\frac{1}{16}''$ from both side edges. Using the $\frac{1}{4}''$ bit, drill $\frac{1}{4}''$-deep horn holes. Angle the bit for the right horn hole towards the bottom of the left cheek and for the left horn hole towards the bottom of the right cheek.

6. Place the body on the work surface. Refer to the photograph at the beginning of the project and the labels on 11–7. With all bottom edges even, glue the legs to the body in the following order: center the right front leg between A and B (the labels on 11–10 show the orientation of this leg to the body), the left front leg between C and D, the left back leg between E and F, and the right back leg between G and H.

7. Glue the neck (11–9) to the body, where indicated by the dashed rectangle on 11–7, so that the neck curves towards the back of the body.

8. Glue the head (11–8) into the notch in the neck (see color photo).

9. Repeat Steps 7 to 13 of the male giraffe. (Don't paint the underside of the body or the underside areas of the legs that touch the work surface.)

Platform

1. Cut an 8″ length of 1×12 pine for the platform.

2. Cut two grasses (11–13) and four grass supports (11–14) from $\frac{1}{4} \times 5\frac{1}{4}$ lattice.

3. On the edge surface of both long sides of the platform, mark for two axle-peg holes, 2″ in from the front edge and 2″ in from the back edge (the short sides) and centered from top to bottom. Using the $\frac{5}{16}''$ bit, drill $\frac{3}{4}''$-deep holes.

4. On the center of the edge surface of one short side, mark for the pull hole. (This is now the front of the platform.) Using the $\frac{3}{16}''$ bit, drill a 1″-deep hole.

5. Place the platform on the work surface with the back facing you. Referring to the photograph at the beginning of the project, stand the male giraffe on the platform. Position the back of his right back hoof $\frac{15}{16}''$ from the back of the platform and $2\frac{1}{16}''$ from the right side. Have the back of his left back hoof $1\frac{9}{16}''$ from the back of the platform. Use a pencil to trace the outline of each hoof onto the platform. Mark the center of each outline for a pilot hole. Using the $\frac{1}{16}''$ bit, drill pilot holes through the platform.

6. Insert the screws from the underside of the platform so that their tips extend slightly above the top surface. Place the male giraffe on the platform, centering his hooves over the screw tips, and pressing slightly to make indentions in the bottom of the hooves. Remove the screws from the platform.

7. Using the $\frac{1}{16}''$ bit, drill a $\frac{3}{4}''$-deep pilot hole into the bottom of each hoof.

8. Place the female giraffe on the platform, as shown in 11–7. (The arrow next to the dashed line on 11–7 indicates the center front of the platform.) Use a pencil to trace the outline of her body and legs.

9. With the bottom edges even, glue the straight side of one grass support (11–14) perpendicular to each side of both grasses, where indicated by the dashed lines on 11–13.

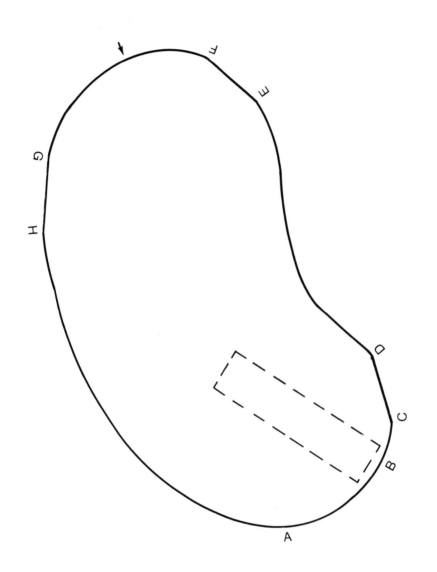

11–7. Female giraffe's body pattern (cut 1) and diagram of the gluing. Positions for the legs and placement of the body on the platform are shown. (Full platform is not shown.)

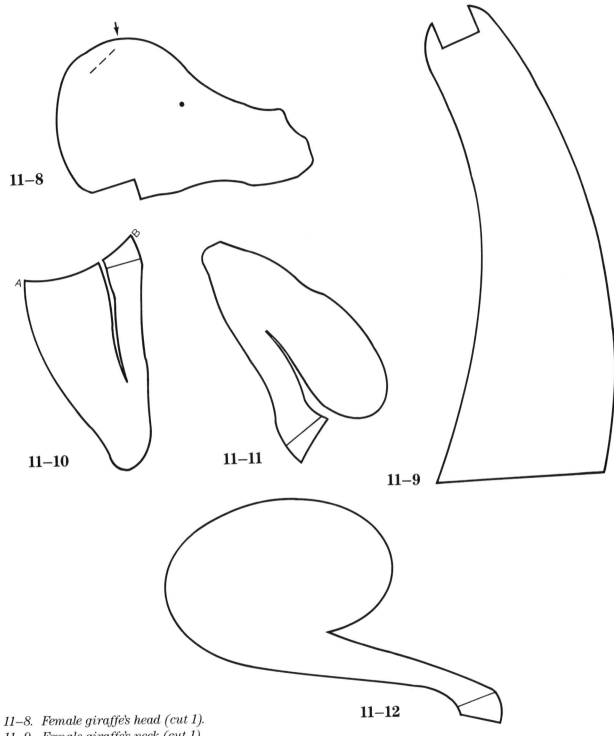

11–8

11–10

11–11

11–9

11–12

11–8. Female giraffe's head (cut 1).
11–9. Female giraffe's neck (cut 1).
11–10. Female giraffe's right-front leg (cut 1).
11–11. Female giraffe's left-front leg (cut 1).
11–12. Female giraffe's back leg (cut 2).

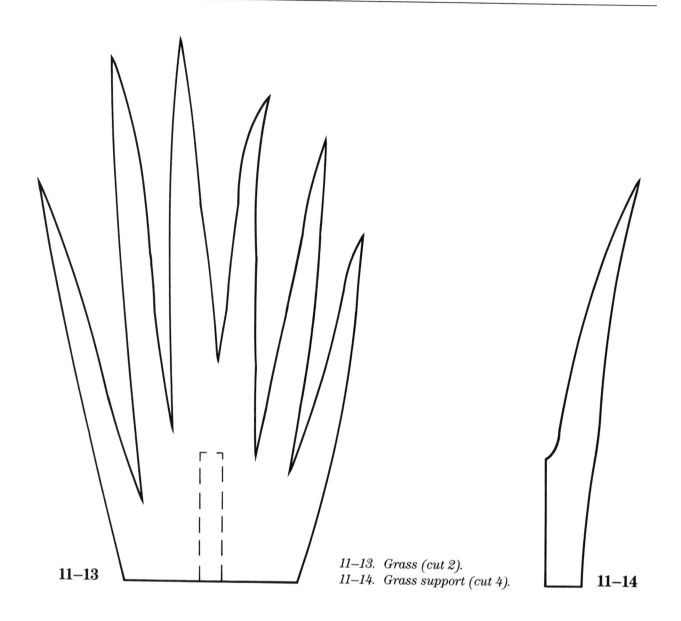

11–13

11–13. *Grass (cut 2).*
11–14. *Grass support (cut 4).*

11–14

10. Place the platform on the work surface with the front facing you. Position one grass assembly so that its widest dimension is parallel with the left side of the platform and its shortest blade faces the front. Have the outside-facing grass support ¾″ from the left side of the platform and the side of the grass 2¹¹⁄₁₆″ from the front. Trace the outline of the base of the grass on the platform with a pencil.

11. Place the platform on the work surface with the back facing you. Position the other grass assembly so that its widest dimension is parallel with the back

of the platform and its shortest blade faces the left. Have the outside-facing grass support ⅞″ from the back of the platform and the side of the grass ⅝″ from the left. Trace the outline of the base of the grass onto the platform with a pencil.

12. Paint the platform medium taupe. (Don't paint into the pilot and axle peg holes or within the outlines of the male's hooves, the female's body and legs, and the grasses.)

13. Paint the grasses medium yellow-green. (Don't paint the underside of the grasses.)

14. Use dark brown to paint the caps of the four 1⅝″-long × ⅜″-diameter wooden axle pegs.

15. Apply glue to the bottom of the male giraffe's hooves, and secure him to the platform with the screws.

16. Glue the female giraffe and the grasses to the platform.

17. Apply the satin finish to the entire assembly, the 1½″-diameter wheel used for the pull knob, the 2½″-diameter wheels, and the axle peg caps.

18. Cut three 6″ lengths of Persian yarn for each giraffe's tail. Gather the strands together and hold them close to one end. Apply tacky glue to that end, and use the toothpick to guide the glued end into a tail hole. Allow to dry; then plait a 3½″-long braid. Use a single ply of yarn to securely wrap the braid 3″ from the tail hole. Tie a knot and cut the wrapping yarn close to the knot. Trim the tail ½″ below the wrapping. Separate and tease the plys at the end of the tail into a fluffy tassel.

19. Cut two 40″ lengths of Persian yarn for each giraffe's mane. Fold the strands in half and hold the cut ends together in one hand. Insert a pencil through the folded end, and rotate the pencil to twist the yarn until it begins to crimp. Fold the yarn in half again, holding the cut ends and pencil in one hand. With your other hand, hold the yarn at the fold and stretch the yarn to straighten the strands. Release that hand with a snapping motion to twist all the strands together.

20. Use a single ply of yarn to securely wrap around the male giraffe's mane 7½″ from the fold. (Knot the female's mane 8¼″ from the fold.) Tie a knot and cut the wrapping yarn close to the knot. Trim the ends ¾″ from the wrapping for the bangs. With the folded end of the mane at the base of the neck, use tacky glue to adhere the mane to the back of the neck and head, ending between the horns. Separate the ends and tease into fluffy bangs.

21. To attach each wheel, apply a small amount of glue into an axle peg hole in the platform. Insert an axle peg through the hole in a wheel, through a washer, and then into the glued axle peg hole in the platform. The wheels should be able to spin freely.

22. Use tacky glue to adhere one end of the boot lace into the pull hole in the platform. Knot the lace 3″ from the free end. Draw the free end through the hole in the pull knob. Knot the free end close to the knob, and trim the end 1″ from the knot.

12. Zebra Hobbyhorse

MATERIALS

- 10″ length of ¼ × 5¼ clear pine lattice
- 10″ length of ½ × 5½ clear pine lattice
- 36″ length of 1 × 12 clear pine
- 2″ length of 2 × 4 clear pine
- 30″ length of ⅞″ dowelling

- Two 1⅝″-long × ⅜″-diameter wooden axle pegs
- Two 2½″-diameter wooden wheels
- One white 25-mm large-hole round wood bead
- One round toothpick

- Drill bits: ⅛″, ⁵⁄₃₂″, ⁵⁄₁₆″, and ⅜″
- Spade bit: ⅞″

- Two #19 × ½″ wire brads
- Four #16 × 1¼″ wire brads
- Two #4 × ¾″ flat-head wood screws
- Two ¼″ flat washers

- One ounce each of black and white 4-ply worsted weight yarns

- Acrylic paints: white, black, and light red-brown
- High-gloss finish

Zebras are found in eastern, central, and southern Africa. There are three kinds of zebra. The largest is the Grevy's zebra, which lives on dry plains and hillsides. The elusive mountain zebra inhabits rocky slopes and is rarely seen. The most common is the plains zebra, which lives on the vast grassy plains in herds that contain as many as 10,000 animals! Just as no two people have the same fingerprints, no two zebras have exactly the same stripe pattern. Zebras stand 41 to 59 inches at the shoulder, weigh between 440 and 880 pounds (200 to 400 kg), and feed exclusively on grasses.

Zebra Hobbyhorse*

1. Cut two 18″ lengths of 1 × 12 pine and glue the faces together to make a bonded piece with a finished size 18″ × 11¼″ × 1½″. Cut one head (12–1) from the bonded wood.

2. Cut two 5″ lengths of ¼ × 5¼ lattice, and stack them on top of two 5″ lengths of ½ × 5½ lattice. With the edges even, secure the stack together with a #16 × 1¼″ brad in each corner. Cut four ears (12–2) from the stacked wood, following the outer line of the pattern. Separate the ears and set the two thicker ears aside.

3. Stack the two thinner ears together with their edges even. Secure them with two #19 × ½″ brads spaced 1½″ in from the ear tip and from the bottom of the ear. Using the ⅜″ bit, drill a hole through the center of the stack and thread the scroll saw blade through the hole. Following the inner line of 12–2,

---

*Refer to the General Directions for the techniques needed to complete this project.

12–1. Reduced pattern for the zebra's head. One box = 1" × 1". Enlarge and cut 1.

cut two ear borders from the stacked wood. Release the saw blade to remove the ear borders.

4. Cut two eyes (12–3) and two upper eyelids (12–4) from ¼ × 5¼ lattice.

5. Glue the ear borders to the thick ears cut in Step 2. The pattern (12–2) shows the left ear; the right ear is a mirror image.

6. Glue the upper eyelids (12–4) to the eyes (12–3) where indicated by the dashed lines. The patterns (12–3 and 12–4) show the left eye; the right eye is a mirror image.

7. Split the 25-mm bead in half for the pupils. With the half-holes held vertically, glue the pupils to the centers of the eyes. Fill the bottom half-holes with paste wood filler, allow to dry, and sand smooth.

8. Using the ⅞″ spade bit, drill a 2¾″-deep dowel hole where indicated by the arrow at the base of the neck on 12–1.

9. Mark the center back of the head and the neck (12–1) for the mane holes. Begin where indicated by the arrow at the forehead and end at the arrow on the back of the neck. Space the holes ½″ apart. Using the ⁵⁄₃₂″ bit, drill ⅜″-deep mane holes.

10. Glue the ear assembly to the sides of the head where indicated by the dashed lines on 12–1.

11. Using the ⅛″ bit, drill pilot holes into the ears where indicated by the stars on 12–2 and ¼″ into the head. Secure the ears with wood screws.

12. Glue the eye assembly to the sides of the head where indicated by the dashed eyelines on 12–1.

13. Use the 2″ length of 2 × 4 for the wheel base. Locate the center of one 1⁷⁄₁₆″ × 3³⁄₁₆″ face, and use the ⅞″ spade bit to drill a 1¼″-deep dowel hole. This is the top of the wheel base.

14. Mark one 1⁷⁄₁₆″ × 2″ face as the front. On the side faces, mark ⁷⁄₁₆″ from the bottom and ⁵⁄₁₆″ from the front. Using the ⁵⁄₁₆″ bit, drill ¾″-deep axle-peg holes (see photo at beginning of project).

15. Glue the ⅞″ dowel into the dowel hole in the wheel base. Then glue the opposite end into the hole in the base of the neck, making sure that the front of the wheel base is facing forward.

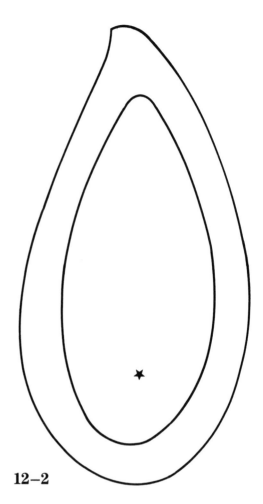

12–2

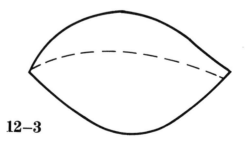

12–3

12–2. Zebra's ear and ear border (cut 4 on outer line).
12–3. Zebra's eye (cut 2).

12–4. Zebra's upper eyelid (cut 2).

16. Being careful not to paint into the mane or axle peg holes, use white to paint the following: white areas of head and neck, upper eyelids, ear borders, underside of ear tips, dowel, wheel base, and axle peg caps. Paint the inner ears, eye irises, pupils, and wheels black. Paint the black areas of the head and neck, extending the stripes onto the edge surfaces.

17. Paint the forehead stripes black and the heart-shaped patch above the nose light red-brown, as shown in 12–5. Paint the nostrils white (see 12–1).

18. Apply the high-gloss finish to all parts.

19. For the mane, cut the yarn into 8″ lengths. Use black yarn where the mane hole is in a black stripe and white yarn where the mane hole is in a white stripe. Place four strands of the same color together, with their edges even, and fold in half. Apply tacky glue into a mane hole. Use the toothpick to guide the folded ends of the yarn into the glued mane hole.

12–5. Front of the zebra's head.

20. To attach each wheel, apply a small amount of glue into an axle peg hole in the wheel base. Insert an axle peg through the hole in a wheel, through a washer, and then into the glued axle peg hole in the base. The wheels should spin freely.

13. Goldfish Bowl

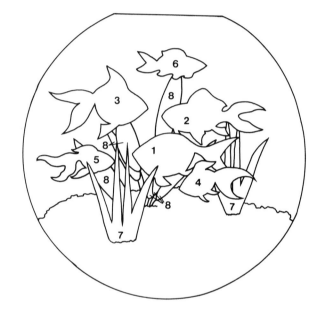

Goldfish are native to East Asia. The Chinese domesticated them 1,000 years ago and over the centuries have bred these naturally greenish-brown or grey fish into 125 colorful and exotic-looking breeds. In captivity, goldfish average from 2 to 4 inches long and can live up to 25 years. When returned to the wild, they grow to their normal size of about 12 inches, but they rarely live longer than 10 years. Key to the photograph: (1–6) goldfish, (7) short grasses, and (8) tall grass patch.

General Directions for Each Goldfish*

1. Using the appropriate patterns, cut one body and two side fins from ¼ × 5¼ lattice.

2. Cut one 1⅜″ × 1½″ stand base from ½ × 5½ lattice.

3. Using the ⅟₁₆″ bit, drill a ⅜″-deep wire-support hole where indicated by the arrow at the bottom of the body.

4. Mark the center of the face of the stand base. Using the ⅟₁₆″ bit, drill a ¼″-deep hole for the wire support.

5. To create each side-fin angle, whittle a flat surface from the dashed line to the star, so that the thickness at the star is less than ⅟₃₂″. The pattern shows the left-side fin; the right-side fin is a mirror image.

---

*Refer to the General Directions section at the beginning of the book for the techniques needed to complete this project.

MATERIALS

- 60″ length of ¼ × 5¼ clear pine lattice
- 10″ length of ½ × 5½ clear pine lattice

- Three white 8-mm regular-hole round wood beads

- Drill bit: ¹⁄₁₆″

- 51″ length of #16 gauge brass wire
- Four #19 × ½″ wire brads

- Wire cutters
- 16″-tall glass-bubble bowl
- 15 pounds of aquarium gravel

- Acrylic paints: medium orange, medium purple, white, black, dark orange, very dark green, and a color to match the gravel
- Acrylic metallic paints: gold, white, and turquoise
- High-gloss finish

6. Glue the side-fin angles to the body where indicated by the dashed lines on the body pattern.

7. To make the eyes for goldfish 1, 2, and 3, cut one 8-mm bead in half for each fish. With the half-holes held horizontally, glue the eyes to the sides of the head where indicated by the dots on the body patterns. (Goldfish 4, 5, and 6 have painted eyes, as shown on their patterns and as described in their painting directions.)

8. Follow the painting directions given for each goldfish, and refer to the color photograph as needed.

9. Apply the high-gloss finish to the goldfish.

10. Paint the stand base to match the gravel.

11. Refer to the table and cut a wire for each goldfish to the length needed to complete the stand.

Table 1. Goldfish Wire Length

Goldfish	Wire length
1	4⅝″
2	6⅜″
3	6¾″
4	3⅝″
5	4¼″
6	8⅝″

12. To assemble, apply tacky glue to both ends of the wire and insert one end into the hole in the bottom of the fish and the other end into the hole in the stand base.

Goldfish #1

1. Use patterns 13–1 and 13–2.

2. Paint the body medium orange. Use medium purple to paint the fins, gills, large spots, and the tail. Paint the small spots gold metallic.

3. Paint the eyes white and the pupils black. Use black to paint the mouth, extending it onto the front edge of the face in an inverted U.

4. Use black to paint the medium spots, gill details, and the details on the bottom back fin and tail. Use black to paint the details (three lines) on the side fins.

Goldfish #2

1. Use patterns 13–3 and 13–4.

2. Use white metallic to paint the lower face, side fins, and the details on the tail and bottom-back fin. Paint the rest of the body, tail, dorsal fin, and bottom back fin medium orange.

3. Paint the eyes white, and the pupils, eye outlines, and gills black. Use black to paint an inverted U-shaped mouth on the front edge of the face ¼″ below the tip of the face.

4. Using gold metallic, paint the patch above the side fins, the dots, and the details on the dorsal fin and tail.

Goldfish #3

1. Use patterns 13–5 and 13–6.

2. Paint the body medium orange. Using gold metallic, paint the fins, tail, gills, and interiors of the scales.

3. Paint the eyes white, and the eye outlines and pupils black. Use black to paint the mouth, extending it onto the front edge of the face in an inverted U.

4. Use black to paint the details on the bottom back fin, tail, and scales. As shown in the color photograph, use black to paint the details (two lines) on the side fins.

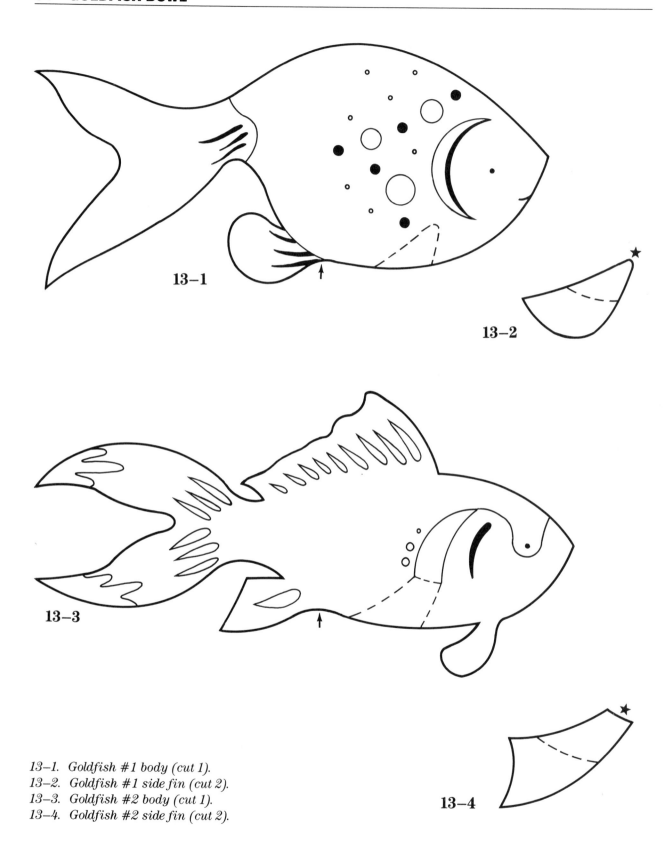

13–1

13–2

13–3

13–4

13–1. *Goldfish #1 body (cut 1).*
13–2. *Goldfish #1 side fin (cut 2).*
13–3. *Goldfish #2 body (cut 1).*
13–4. *Goldfish #2 side fin (cut 2).*

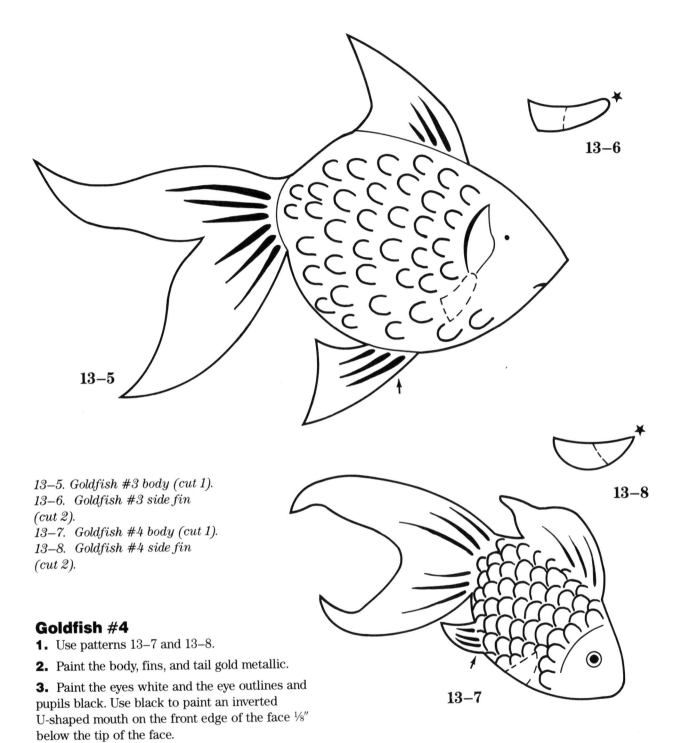

13–5. *Goldfish #3 body (cut 1).*
13–6. *Goldfish #3 side fin*
(cut 2).
13–7. *Goldfish #4 body (cut 1).*
13–8. *Goldfish #4 side fin*
(cut 2).

Goldfish #4

1. Use patterns 13–7 and 13–8.

2. Paint the body, fins, and tail gold metallic.

3. Paint the eyes white and the eye outlines and pupils black. Use black to paint an inverted U-shaped mouth on the front edge of the face ⅛″ below the tip of the face.

4. Use black to paint the gills and the details on the bottom back fin, tail, and scales. As shown in the color photograph, use black to paint the details (three lines) on the side fins.

13–9

13–10

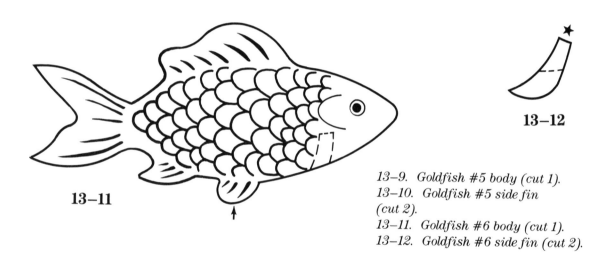

13–11

13–12

13–9. Goldfish #5 body (cut 1).
13–10. Goldfish #5 side fin
(cut 2).
13–11. Goldfish #6 body (cut 1).
13–12. Goldfish #6 side fin (cut 2).

Goldfish #5

1. Use patterns 13–9 and 13–10.

2. Paint the body, fins, and tail gold metallic.

3. Paint the eyes white, and the eye outlines and the pupils black. Use black to paint inside the mouth.

4. Use black to paint the gills and the details on the bottom-back fin, tail, and scales. As shown in the color photograph, use black to paint the details (three lines) on the side fins.

Goldfish #6

1. Use patterns 13–11 and 13–12.

2. Paint the body, fins, and tail medium orange.

3. Paint the eyes white and the eye outlines and pupils black. Use black to paint an inverted U-shaped mouth on the front edge of the face $1/16''$ below the tip of the face.

4. Use dark orange to paint the gills, scales, and the details on the tail and bottom back fin. As shown in the color photograph, use dark orange to paint the details (three lines) on the side fins.

5. Use white metallic to underline the gills and scales. Between each dark orange detail on the fins and tail, paint a shorter white-metallic detail.

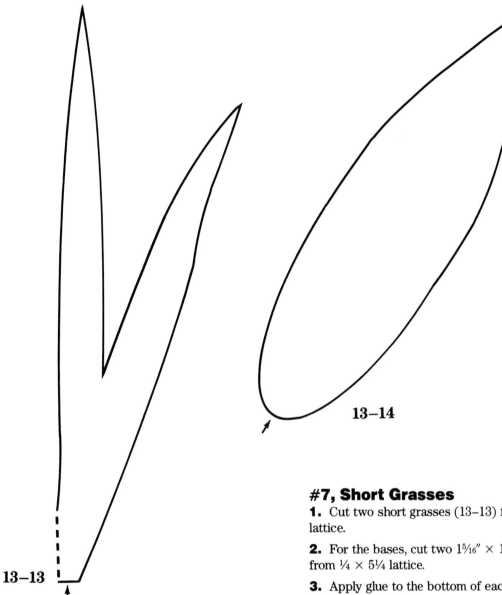

13–13. *Half-pattern for #7, the short grass
(cut 2).*
13–14. *Large grass blade for #8, the tall
grass patch (cut 5).*

#7, Short Grasses

1. Cut two short grasses (13–13) from $\frac{1}{4} \times 5\frac{1}{4}$ lattice.

2. For the bases, cut two $1\frac{5}{16}'' \times 1\frac{1}{2}''$ rectangles from $\frac{1}{4} \times 5\frac{1}{4}$ lattice.

3. Apply glue to the bottom of each grass and center it over a base. Nail brads through the base and into the grass where indicated by the arrows on 13–13.

4. Paint the grasses very dark green, and paint the bases to match the gravel.

5. Apply the high-gloss finish.

#8, Tall Grass Patch

1. Cut five large grass blades (13–14) and two small grass blades (13–15) from $\frac{1}{4} \times 5\frac{1}{4}$ lattice.

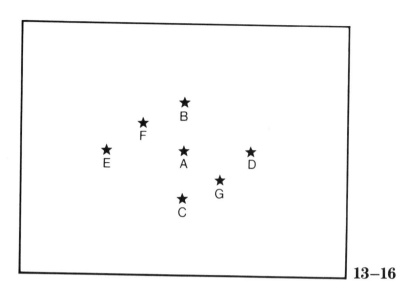

13–15

13–15. Small grass blade for #8, the tall grass patch (cut 2).
13–16. Base for #8, the tall grass patch (cut 1).

2. Cut one base (13–16) from ½ × 5½ lattice.

3. Using the ¹⁄₁₆″ bit, drill a ⅜″-deep stem hole in the bottom of each grass blade where indicated by the arrows on 13–14 and 13–15.

4. Using the ¹⁄₁₆″ bit, drill ¼″-deep stem holes into the base where indicated by the stars on 13–16.

5. Paint the grass blades turquoise metallic, and paint the base to match the gravel.

6. Refer to Table 2 to match the stem-hole letter on the base (13–16) to the corresponding grass-blade size and to the wire length needed for the stem.

7. To assemble, apply tacky glue to both ends of each stem and insert one end into the stem hole of the grass blade and the other end into the corresponding hole in the base. As shown in the photograph, bend the stems of grass blades B–G into curves so that they arch away from grass blade A at the center.

Assembling the Bowl

Pour the gravel into the bowl. Bury the bases in the gravel. See the photograph for a suggested arrangement.

Table 2. Grass Blade Size and Wire Length

Base letter	Grass-blade size	Wire length
A	Large	4½″
B	Small	3″
C	Small	2⅜″
D	Large	1⅛″
E	Large	1⅝″
F	Large	2⅜″
G	Large	1½″

14. Greater Pandas

Greater pandas live only in the remote mountain forests at the center of the People's Republic of China. Weighing just 5 ounces (140 gm) at birth, pandas grow to 5 feet tall and weigh between 250 and 300 pounds (114 and 136 kg). They eat mainly bamboo and consume about 20 pounds (9 kg) of it a day! In danger of extinction in the wild, the panda was chosen by the World Wildlife Fund as its symbol for all endangered animals.

Mother Panda*

1. Cut two 10″ lengths of 1 × 6 pine and glue the faces together to form a bonded piece with a finished size of 10″ × 5½″ × 1½″. Cut one body (14–1) and one head (14–2) from the bonded wood.

2. Cut two front legs (14–3) and two back legs (14–4) from ½ × 5½ lattice.

3. Cut two ears (14–5) and one nose (14–6) from ¼ × 2⅝ lattice.

4. Using the ²³⁄₆₄″ bit, drill a ¾″-deep neck hole into

---

*Refer to the General Directions for the techniques needed to complete this project.

---

the body (14–1) and into the head (14–2), where indicated by the arrows.

5. Using the ⁵⁄₁₆″ bit, drill ½″-deep axle peg holes, where indicated by the stars, on both sides of the body (14–1). Then drill axle peg holes, where indicated by the stars, through the front and back legs (14–3 and 14–4).

6. Use the 1½″ length of ⅜″ dowelling for the neck peg.

7. Apply glue to the neck peg, and insert it into the hole in the head.

8. Whittle the upper edge of each ear to a 60° angle, working from the dashed line to the straight edge.

9. Glue the ear angles to the sides of the head where indicated by the dashed lines on 14–2. The ears should angle towards the back of the head, as shown in 14–7.

10. Whittle the nose, as shown in 14–7, to form nostrils. Whittle the underside of the nose as needed to fit the contour of the face. Glue the nose between the squares on the head (14–2).

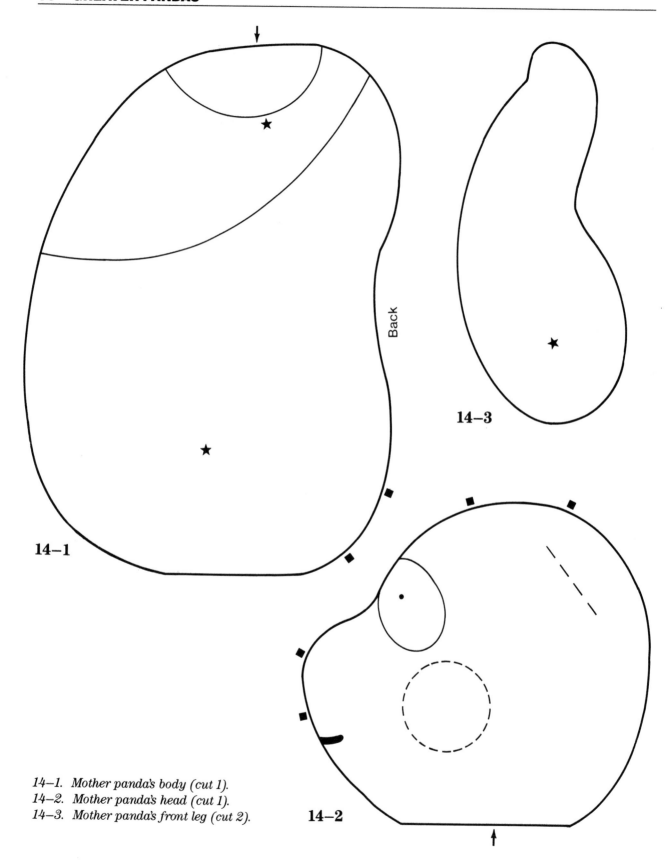

Back

14–3

14–1

14–2

14–1. *Mother panda's body (cut 1).*
14–2. *Mother panda's head (cut 1).*
14–3. *Mother panda's front leg (cut 2).*

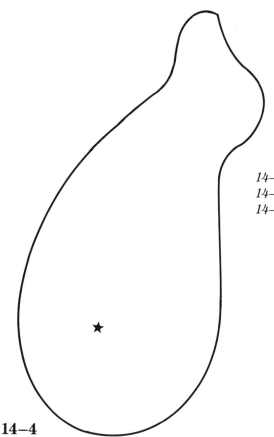

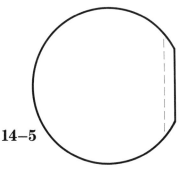

14—5

14—6

14—4. Mother panda's back leg (cut 2).
14—5. Mother panda's ear (cut 2).
14—6. Mother panda's nose (cut 1).

14—4

11. Split a 10-mm bead in half for the eyes. With the half-holes parallel with the forehead, glue the eyes to the head where indicated by the dots on 14–2.

12. Split the 25-mm bead in half for the cheeks. With the half-holes held horizontal, glue the cheeks to the head where indicated by the dashed lines on 14–2. Fill the half-holes with paste wood filler, allow to dry, and sand smooth.

13. Trim ¼" from the ends of the ⅜"-diameter axle pegs so that each measures 1⅜" from the top of the cap to the bottom of the peg.

14. Paint the body and head white. (Don't paint the neck peg or into the neck and axle peg holes.) Use black to paint the body band, eyes, eye rings, ears, nose, legs, and axle peg caps. Extend the body band onto the front and back edges of the body.

14—7. Mother and baby panda, close-up of faces.

15. Referring to 14–7, paint the mouth black and the tongue medium pink, and use white to highlight each eye.

16. Apply the high-gloss finish to all parts.

17. To attach each leg, apply a small amount of glue into a peg hole in the body. Insert an axle peg through the peg hole in a corresponding leg and then into the glued peg hole in the body. The legs should be able to move up and down and hold a pose.

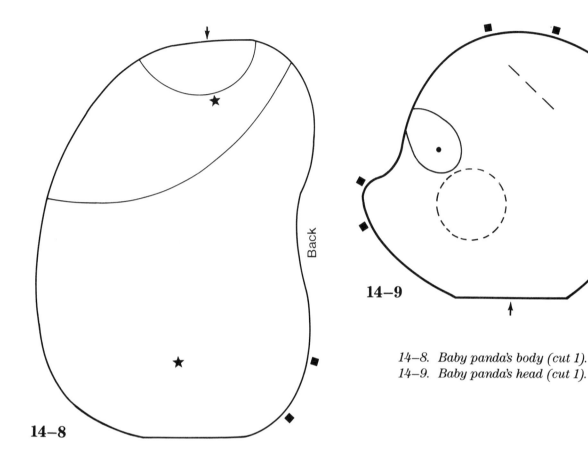

14—9

14—8

14—8. Baby panda's body (cut 1).
14—9. Baby panda's head (cut 1).

18. For the head fur, cut a 1″ × 1¼″ rectangle of fake fur. Trim the corners to round them. Use tacky glue to adhere the fur between the squares on top of the head (14–2).

19. For the tail, cut a ¾″-diameter circle of fake fur. Use tacky glue to adhere the tail between the squares on the body (14–1).

20. To attach the head, insert the neck peg into the neck hole in the top of the body (do not glue). The head should be able to move from right to left.

Baby Panda

1. Cut two 8″ lengths of ½ × 5½ lattice and glue the faces together to form a bonded piece with a finished size of 8″ × 5⁷⁄₁₆″ × ¹⁵⁄₁₆″. Cut one body (14–8) and one head (14–9) from the bonded wood.

2. Cut two front legs (14–10) and two back legs (14–11) from ½ × 5½ lattice.

3. Cut two ears (14–12) and one nose (14–13) from ¼ × 2⅝ lattice.

4. Using the ¹⁵⁄₆₄″ bit, drill a ¾″-deep neck hole into the body (14–8) and into the head (14–9), where indicated by the arrows.

5. Using the ⁷⁄₃₂″ bit, drill ⅜″-deep axle peg holes, where indicated by the stars, on both sides of the body (14–8). Then drill axle peg holes, where indicated by the stars, through the front and back legs (14–10 and 14–11).

6. Use the 1½″ length of ¼″ dowelling for the neck peg.

7. Repeat Steps 7 to 11 of the mother panda.

8. Split the 20-mm bead in half for the cheeks. With the half-holes held horizontal, glue the cheeks to the head where indicated by the dashed lines on 14–9. Fill the half-holes with paste wood filler, allow it to dry, and sand it smooth.

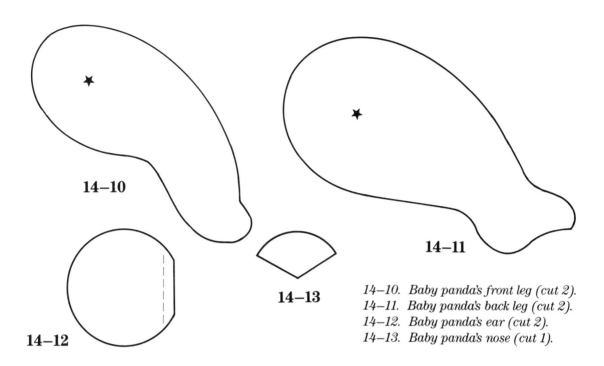

14–10
14–11
14–13
14–12

14–10. Baby panda's front leg (cut 2).
14–11. Baby panda's back leg (cut 2).
14–12. Baby panda's ear (cut 2).
14–13. Baby panda's nose (cut 1).

9. Trim ⅛″ from the ends of the ¼″-diameter axle pegs so that each measures 1⅛″ from the top of the cap to the bottom of the peg.

10. Repeat Steps 14 to 17 of the mother panda instructions.

11. For the head fur, cut a ⅝″ × ⅞″ rectangle of fake fur. Trim the corners to round them. Trim the fur so it's ¾″ long. Use tacky glue to adhere the fur between the squares on top of the head (14–9).

12. For the tail, cut a ⅝″-diameter circle of fake fur. Trim the fur so it's ¾″ long. Use tacky glue to adhere the tail between the squares on the body (14–8).

13. Repeat Step 20 of the mother panda instructions.

15. Tiger Hobbyhorse

MATERIALS

- 2″ length of ¼ × 5¼ clear pine lattice
- 10″ length of ½ × 5½ clear pine lattice
- 36″ length of 1 × 12 clear pine
- 2″ length of 2 × 4 clear pine
- 36″ length of ⅞″ dowelling

- Two 1⅝″-long × ⅜″-diameter wooden axle pegs
- Two 2½″-diameter wooden wheels
- One white 20-mm large-hole round wood bead

- Drill bit: ⁵⁄₁₆″
- Spade bit: ⅞″

- Two ¼″ flat washers

- Whitewash brush bristles
- Small amount of white fake fur
- Acrylic paints: medium orange (MO), white (W), pale yellow (PY), black (B), dark yellow (DY), dark red-brown (DRB), and terra cotta (TC)
- High-gloss finish

Tiger Hobbyhorse*

1. Cut two 18″ lengths of 1 × 12 pine and glue the faces together to form one bonded piece with a finished size of 18″ × 11¼″ × 1½″. Cut one head (15–1) from the bonded wood.

2. Cut one nose (15–2) and one lower lip (15–3) from ¼ × 5¼ lattice.

3. Cut two ears (15–4) and two cheeks (15–5) from ½ × 5½ lattice. The patterns show the orientation for the right ear and cheek; the left ear and cheek are mirror images.

4. Using the ⅞″ spade bit, drill a 2″-deep dowel hole where indicated by the arrow on 15–1.

---

*Refer to the General Directions for the techniques needed to complete this project.

Tigers are the largest member of the cat family and inhabit forests, wooded hillsides, and swamps in various parts of Asia. Solitary animals, they spend most of the day resting and sleeping in the shade, and most of the night hunting and eating. Tigers usually feed on deer, wild cattle, and wild pigs. About the size of a large kitten at birth, they grow to be 7 to 9 feet long from nose to tail and weigh between 240 and 500 pounds (109 and 227 kg).

5. Using the ¹⁄₁₆″ bit, drill ¼″-deep whisker holes where indicated by the stars on 15–1.

6. Whittle the upper edge of each ear to a 55° angle, working from the dashed line to the straight edge (15–4).

7. Glue the ear angles to the sides of the head where indicated by the dashed lines on 15–1. The

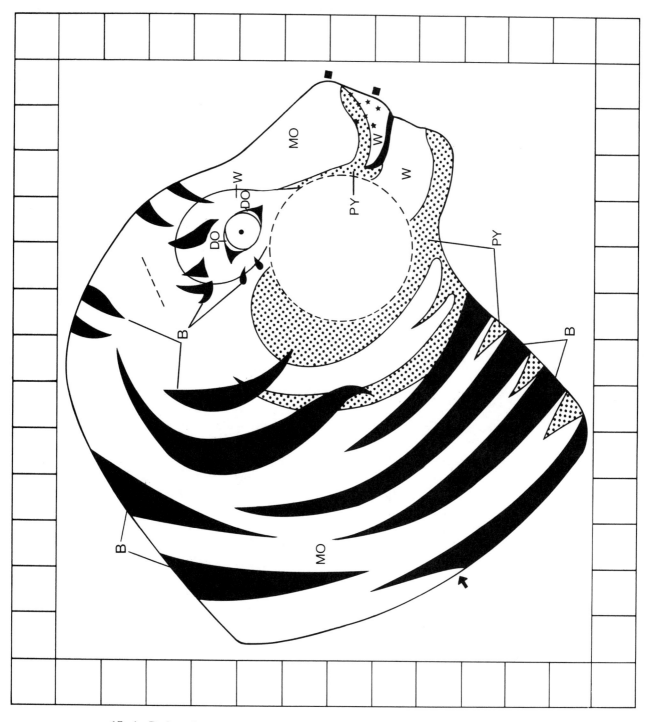

15–1. Reduced pattern for the tiger's head. One box = 1" × 1". Enlarge and cut 1.

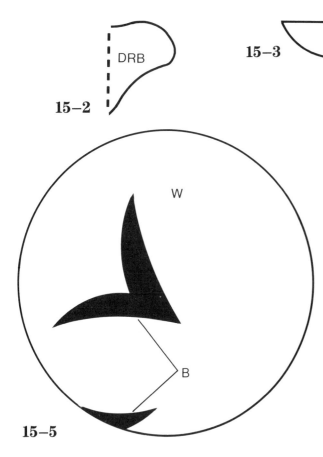

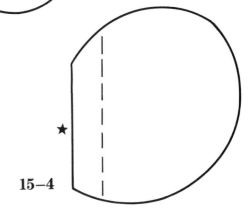

15–2. Half-pattern for the tiger's nose (cut 1).
15–3. Tiger's lower lip (cut 1).
15–4. Tiger's ear (cut 2).
15–5. Tiger's cheek (cut 2).

ears should angle towards the back of the head, as shown in 15–7.

8. Split the 20-mm bead in half for the pupils. With the half-holes held horizontally, glue the pupils to the sides of the head where indicated by the dots on 15–1. Fill the half-holes with paste wood filler, allow it to dry, and sand it smooth.

9. Glue the cheeks (15–5) to the sides of the head where indicated by the dashed circles on 15–1.

10. Glue the nose and lower lip to the front of the head. Position the nose between the squares on 15–1 and the lower lip below the mouth.

11. Use the 2″ length of 2 × 4 for the wheel base. Locate the center of one 1⅞6″ × 3³⁄₁₆″ face, and use the ⅞″ spade bit to drill a 1¼″-deep dowel hole. This is the top of the wheel base.

12. Mark one 1⅞6″ × 2″ face of the wheelbase as the front. On the side faces, mark ⅞6″ from the bottom and ⁵⁄₁₆″ from the front. Using the ⁵⁄₁₆″ bit, drill ¾″-deep axle peg holes.

13. Glue the ⅞″ dowel in the dowel hole in the wheel base. Then glue the opposite end into the hole in the base of the neck, making sure that the front of the wheel base is facing forwards.

14. Referring to the Materials list for the colors, paint the head as shown on 15–1 and the color photograph. Paint the cheeks as shown on 15–5. Extend the colors onto the edge surfaces, and paint the stripe details shown in 15–6 and 15–7. Use black to paint the eye outlines, pupils, and mouth.

15. Paint the backs and edges of the ears medium orange. On the front of each ear, paint a ⁵⁄₁₆″-wide white outer band, a ¼″-wide pale yellow inner band, and a black center. (See the color photograph.)

16. Referring to 15–6, paint the nose dark red-brown and the lower lip terra cotta. Use black to paint the nostrils, the muzzle detail, and the front view of the mouth and to outline the whisker holes.

17. Paint the wheels medium orange, and use black to paint the dowel, wheel base, and axle peg caps.

18. Apply the high-gloss finish to all parts.

19. Cut one right neck ruff (15–8) from fake fur. Turn the pattern over and cut one left neck ruff. Apply tacky glue to the neck ruffs and adhere them

15–6. Front of the tiger's head.

15–7. Back of the tiger's head.

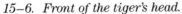

15–8. Tiger's right neck ruff. (Cut 1, turn the pattern over, and cut 1 left neck ruff.)

to the neck and head, beginning at the center front of the neck and ending at the back of the cheeks.

20. Cut a 1⅛″-diameter half-circle of fake fur. Adhere it with tacky glue below the lower lip.

21. Cut fifty-six 3½″-long bristles from a whitewash brush for the whiskers. Gather four whiskers at a time together and hold them close to one end. Dip

that end into tacky glue and insert it into a whisker hole. Repeat for the other holes.

22. To attach each wheel, apply a small amount of glue into an axle peg hole in the wheel base. Insert an axle peg through the hole in a wheel, through a washer, and then into the glued axle peg hole in the base. The wheels should spin freely.

16. Asian Elephant Pull Toy

MATERIALS

- 20″ length of ¼ × 5¼ clear pine lattice
- 30″ length of ½ × 5½ clear pine lattice
- 8″ length of 1 × 12 clear pine
- 10″ length of ⁵⁄₄ × 12 clear pine
- 5″ length of ¼″ dowelling

- Four 1⅝″-long × ⅜″-diameter wooden axle pegs
- One 1½″-diameter wooden wheel
- Four 2½″-diameter wooden wheels
- Two white 8-mm regular-hole round wood beads
- One white 10-mm regular-hole round wood bead

- Drill bits: ¹⁄₁₆″, ⅛″, ³⁄₁₆″, and ⁵⁄₁₆″

- Four #6 × 1½″ flat-head wood screws
- Sixteen #19 × ½″ wire brads
- Eight #18 × 1″ wire brads
- Four ¼″ flat washers

- Scrap of medium-grey synthetic suede
- Ten 5″ lengths of natural or plastic raffia
- 36″ length of cotton clothesline

- Acrylic paint: dark grey, black, white, light grey, medium grey, terra cotta, and light moss-green
- High-gloss finish

Elephants are the largest of all living land animals. Asian elephants are 6 to 8 feet high at the shoulder (about 2 feet less than their African kin) and weigh 3 to 5 tons (2.7 to 4.5 metric tons). At birth, babies stand 3 feet tall and weigh 200 pounds (91 kg). Only male Asian elephants grow tusks. Tusk length can be uneven, because an elephant may favor one tusk more than the other when prying off tree bark and digging up roots. Asian elephants have been used as work animals for thousands of years. A few remain in the wild in the grasslands and forests of India and Southeast Asia.

Father Elephant*

1. Cut one body (16–1) from ⁵⁄₄ × 12 pine.

2. Cut two front legs (16–2) and two back legs (16–3) from ½ × 5½ lattice.

3. Cut two ears (16–4) from ¼ × 5¼ lattice. The pattern shows the orientation of the left ear; the right ear is a mirror image.

4. Using the ³⁄₁₆″ bit, drill a ¼″-deep tail hole where indicated by the arrow on 16–1.

5. Using two #18 × 1″ brads for each leg, glue and nail the legs to the body where indicated by the dashed lines on 16–1. (The leg positions are the same for both sides of the body.) Make sure that the feet rest flat on the work surface.

6. Whittle the underside of each ear (16–4) to a 45° angle, working from the dashed line to the star.

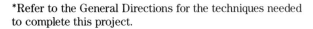

*Refer to the General Directions for the techniques needed to complete this project.

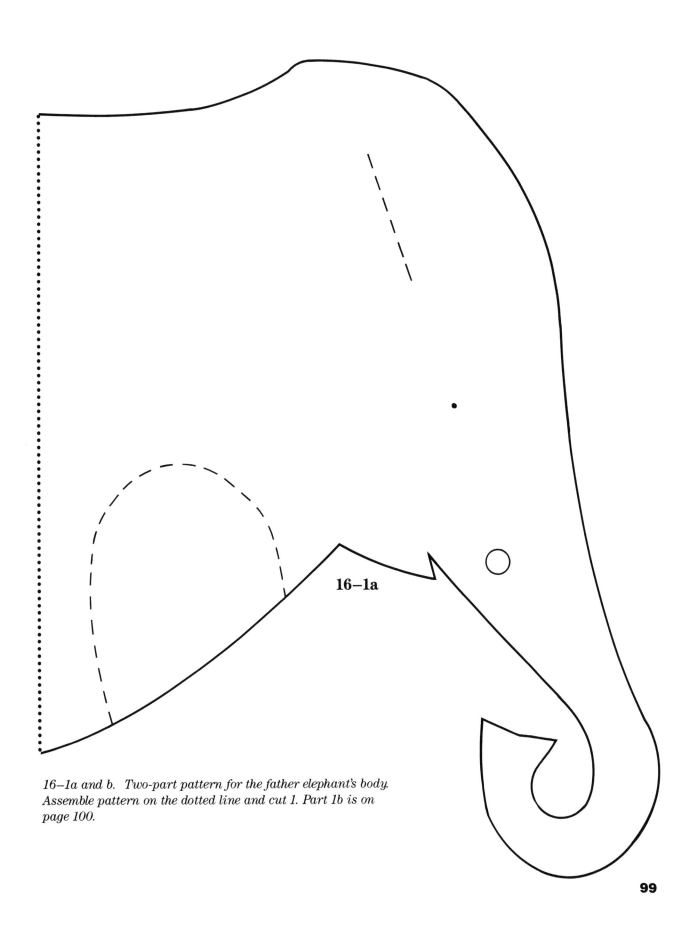

16-1a

16–1a and b. Two-part pattern for the father elephant's body.
Assemble pattern on the dotted line and cut 1. Part 1b is on
page 100.

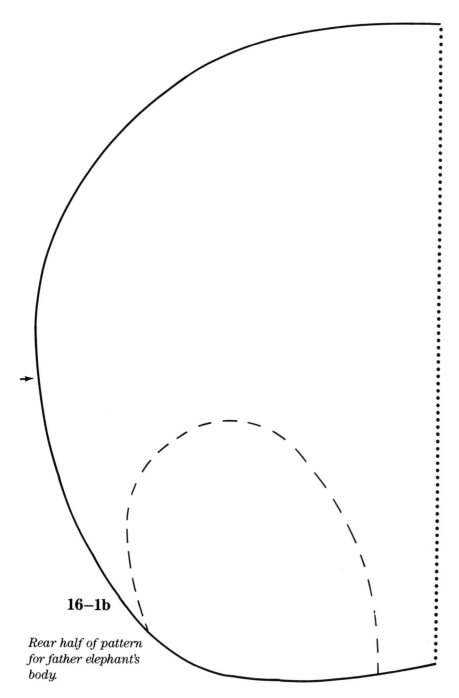

16–1b

*Rear half of pattern
for father elephant's
body.*

7. Glue the ear angles to the sides of the head where indicated by the dashed lines on 16–1.

8. Use the 5″ length of ¼″ dowelling for the tusks. To indicate the angle of the tusk cut, mark 1½″ from the right end. Rotate the dowelling so that the mark is away from you, and then mark 1½″ from the left

end; saw from mark to mark. Whittle ¾″ of the flat end of each tusk to a point.

9. Glue the angled end of each tusk to the upper trunk where indicated by the large circles on 16–1. The tusks should point out and slightly down.

10. Split the 10-mm bead in half for the eyes. With

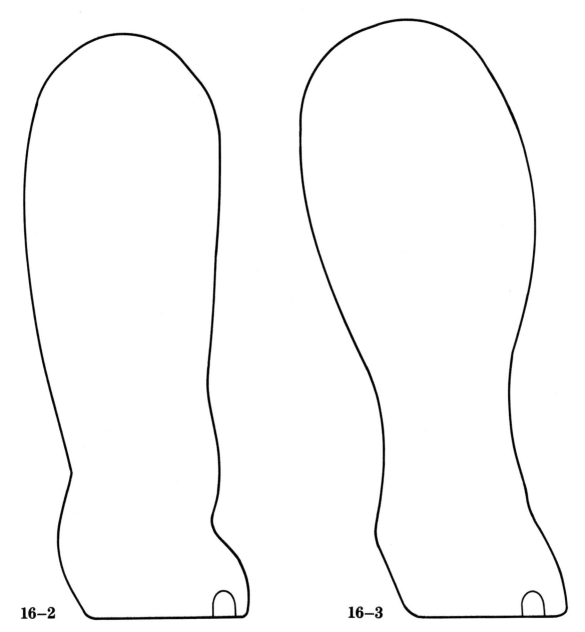

16–2. Father elephant's front leg (cut 2).
16–3. Father elephant's back leg (cut 2).

the half-holes held parallel with the tusks, glue the eyes to the sides of the head where indicated by the dots on 16–1.

11. Paint the body dark grey. (Don't paint the bottom of the feet.) Use black to paint the eyes and a ⅞″ × ½″ rectangle in the center of the flat end of the trunk. Use white to highlight the right eye at 4 o'clock and the left eye at 8 o'clock. Paint the tusks white. Paint the toenails white, painting a third toenail (matching the others) at the center front of each foot.

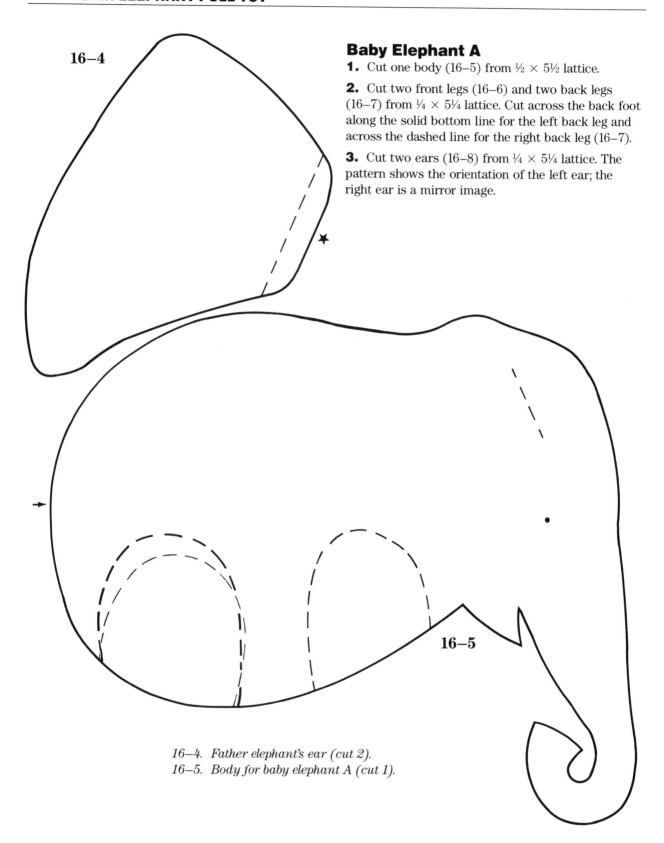

16–4

Baby Elephant A

1. Cut one body (16–5) from ½ × 5½ lattice.

2. Cut two front legs (16–6) and two back legs (16–7) from ¼ × 5¼ lattice. Cut across the back foot along the solid bottom line for the left back leg and across the dashed line for the right back leg (16–7).

3. Cut two ears (16–8) from ¼ × 5¼ lattice. The pattern shows the orientation of the left ear; the right ear is a mirror image.

16–5

16–4. Father elephant's ear (cut 2).
16–5. Body for baby elephant A (cut 1).

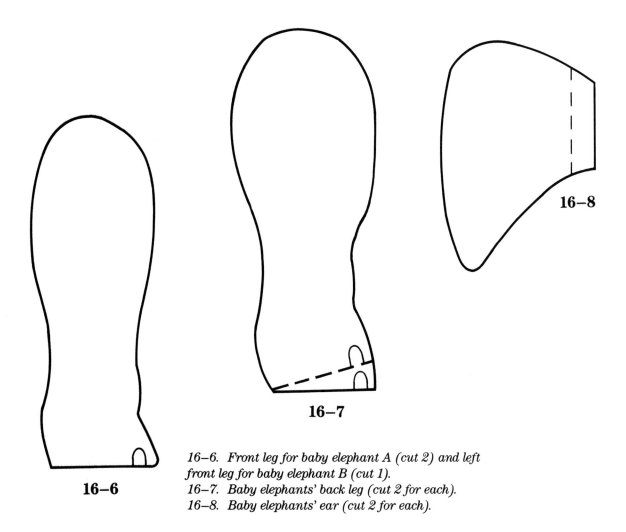

16–6. *Front leg for baby elephant A (cut 2) and left front leg for baby elephant B (cut 1).*
16–7. *Baby elephants' back leg (cut 2 for each).*
16–8. *Baby elephants' ear (cut 2 for each).*

4. Using the ⅛" bit, drill a ¼"-deep tail hole where indicated by the arrow on the body.

5. Using two #19 × ½" brads for each leg, glue and nail the front legs (the same front leg position is used on both sides of the body) and the right back leg to the body where indicated by the light dashed lines (16–5). Glue and nail the left back leg to the body where indicated by the heavy dashed line. Make sure that the feet rest flat on the work surface.

6. Whittle the underside of each ear (16–8) to a 45° angle, working from the dashed line to the straight edge.

7. Glue the ear angles to the sides of the head where indicated by the dashed lines on the body pattern (16–5).

8. Split an 8-mm bead in half for the eyes. With the half-holes held horizontally, glue the eyes to the sides of the head where indicated by the dots on 16–5.

9. Paint the body light grey. (Don't paint the underside of the feet.) Paint the eyes black. Use white to highlight the right eye at 5 o'clock and the left eye at 7 o'clock. Paint the toenails white, painting a third toenail (matching the others) at the center front of each foot.

10. Using dark grey, paint a ⁵⁄₁₆" × ⅜" rectangle in the center of the flat end of the trunk.

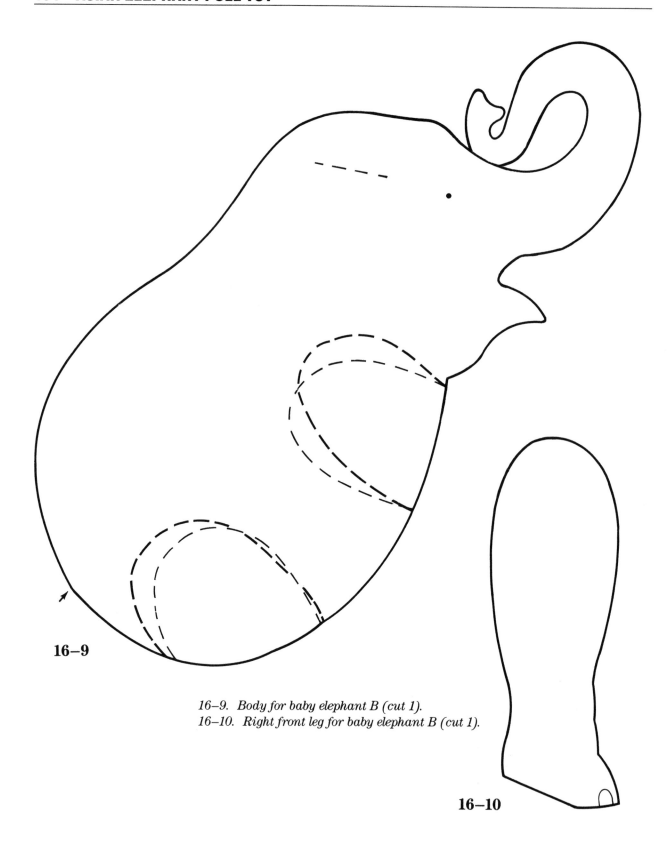

16—9

16—10

16–9. Body for baby elephant B (cut 1).
16–10. Right front leg for baby elephant B (cut 1).

Baby Elephant B

1. Cut one body (16–9) from ½ × 5½ lattice.

2. Cut one right front leg (16–10), one left front leg (16–6), and two back legs (16–7) from ¼ × 5¼ lattice. Cut across the foot along the solid bottom line for the left back leg and across the dashed line for the right back leg.

3. Repeat Steps 3 and 4 of baby elephant A.

4. Using two #19 × ½″ brads for each leg, glue and nail the right front and right back legs to the body (16–9) where indicated by the light dashed lines and the left front and left back legs where indicated by the heavy dashed lines. Make sure that the feet rest flat on the work surface.

5. Repeat Steps 6 to 9 of baby elephant A, but paint the body medium grey.

6. Using dark grey, paint a ⅜″ × ¼″ rectangle in the center of the flat end of the trunk. Paint the mouth opening terra cotta, leaving a ⅛″ border of medium grey on all sides.

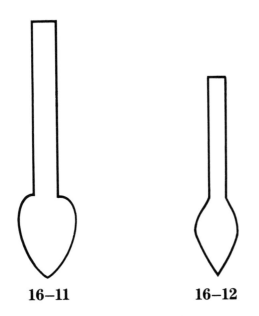

16–11   **16–12**

16–11. Father elephant's tail (cut 1).
16–12. Baby elephants' tail (cut 1 for each).

Platform

1. Use the 8″ length of 1 × 12 pine for the platform.

2. On the edge surface of both long sides of the platform, mark for two axle peg holes, 2⅛″ in from the front and back edges (the short sides) and centered from top to bottom. Using the 5⁄16″ bit, drill ¾″-deep holes.

3. In the center of the edge surface of one short side, mark for the pull hole. (This is now the front of the platform.) Using the 3⁄16″ bit, drill a 1″-deep hole at the mark.

4. Place the platform on the work surface with the back facing you. Referring to the photograph at the beginning of the project, stand the father elephant on the platform. Position the tip of his left front foot 3⅝″ from the front of the platform and 1⅛″ in from the left side. Have the center of his left back foot ⅞″ from the left side. Use a pencil to trace the outline of each foot onto the platform. Mark the center of each outline for a pilot hole. Using the 1⁄16″ bit, drill pilot holes through the platform.

5. Insert the screws from the underside of the platform so that their tips extend slightly above the top. Place the father elephant on the platform, centering his feet over the screw tips, and press slightly to make indentions in the bottom of the feet. Remove the screws from the platform.

6. Using the 1⁄16″ bit, drill a ¾″-deep pilot hole into the bottom of each foot at the indentions marked in Step 5.

7. Place the platform on the work surface with the back facing you. Referring to the photograph, stand baby elephant B on the platform. Position the tip of his right front foot 3¾″ from the front edge and 1¾″ in from the right side. Have the center of his left back foot 3⅜″ from the right side. Use a pencil to trace the outline of each foot onto the platform.

8. With the platform in the same position, stand baby elephant A on the platform. Position the tip of her right front foot 8⅛″ from the front edge and 1⅛″ from the right side. Have the center of her left back foot 3″ from the right side. Trace the outline of each foot. Apply glue to the bottom of the feet, and adhere both baby elephants to the platform where indicated by the pencil lines.

9. Paint the platform light moss-green. (Don't paint

into the pilot holes and axle peg holes or within the outlines of the father elephant's feet.)

10. Apply glue to the bottom of the father elephant's feet, and secure him to the platform with the screws.

11. Use terra cotta to paint the 1½"-diameter wheel used for the pull knob and the axle peg caps.

12. Apply the high-gloss finish to the entire assembly, the pull knob, the 2½"-diameter wheels, and the axle peg caps.

13. Cut one father's tail (16–11) and two baby's tails (16–12) from grey synthetic suede. Use tacky glue to adhere the end of each tail into the appropriate tail hole in a body.

14. Gather the raffia into a bundle, with its edges even. Use tacky glue to adhere it to the trunk curl of baby elephant B, as shown in the photograph.

15. To attach each wheel, apply a small amount of glue into an axle peg hole in the platform. Insert an axle peg through the hole in a wheel, through a washer, and then into the glued axle peg hole in the platform. The wheels should be able to spin freely.

16. Use tacky glue to adhere one end of the clothesline into the pull hole in the platform. Knot the clothesline 3" from the free end. Draw the free end through the hole in the pull knob. Knot the free end close to the knob, and trim the end close to the knot.

17. Koalas

- 10″ length of ¼ × 1⅜ clear pine lattice
- 18″ length of ½ × 5½ clear pine lattice
- 12″ length of 1 × 8 clear pine
- 5″ length of ¼″ dowelling

- Eight 1¼″-long × ¼″-diameter wooden axle pegs
- Two white 8-mm regular-hole round wood beads

- Drill bits: $\frac{7}{32}$″ and $\frac{15}{64}$″

- Small amount of reddish-brown fake fur

- Acrylic paints: light grey-brown, black, white, dark brown, beige, and medium pink
- High-gloss finish

Koalas*

The following directions are for one koala. The variations needed for the second koala are given in brackets.

1. Cut one body (17–1) and one head (17–2) from 1 × 8 pine.

2. Cut one right front leg (17–3), one left front leg (17–4), and two back legs (17–5) from ½ × 5½ lattice. [Reverse the front legs for the second koala.]

3. Cut two ears (17–6) and one nose (17–7) from ¼ × 1⅜ lattice.

4. Using the $\frac{15}{64}$″ bit, drill a ¾″-deep neck hole into the body (17–1) and into the head (17–2), where indicated by the arrows.

5. Using the $\frac{7}{32}$″ bit, drill $\frac{5}{16}$″-deep axle peg holes, where indicated by the stars, on both sides of the

Koalas are found in the forests of eastern Australia, where they live in trees and rarely descend to the ground. These slow-moving animals are only active for about 4 hours each night and then sleep or rest the remainder of the time. Their diet consists solely of eucalyptus leaves and bark. Commonly called koala bears, they are not related to bears at all, but are marsupials. Marsupials are mammals whose young are very tiny when born. They make their way to their mother's pouch and remain there until they are more fully developed. Although only the size of a grape at birth, koalas grow 24 to 33 inches tall and weigh about 20 pounds (9 kg).

*Refer to the General Directions for the techniques needed to complete this project.

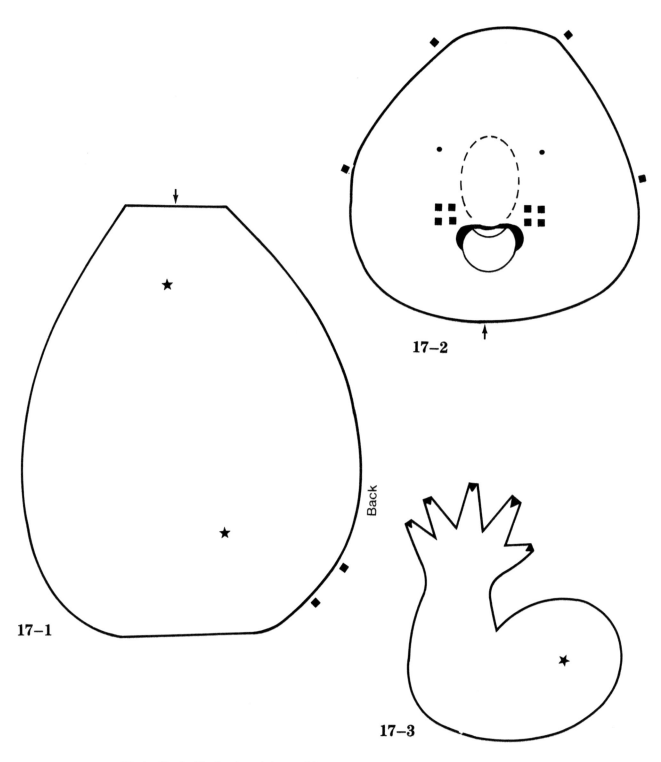

17–2

Back

17–1

17–3

17–1. *Koalas' body (cut 1 for each).*
17–2. *Koalas' head (cut 1 for each).*
17–3. *Koalas' right front leg (cut 1 for each).*

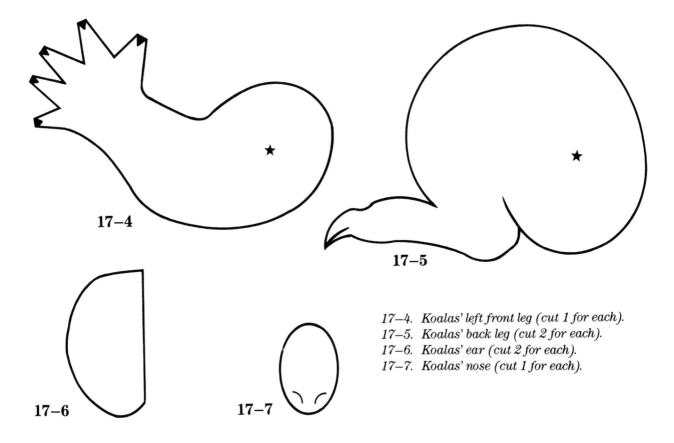

17–4

17–5

17–6

17–7

17–4. Koalas' left front leg (cut 1 for each).
17–5. Koalas' back leg (cut 2 for each).
17–6. Koalas' ear (cut 2 for each).
17–7. Koalas' nose (cut 1 for each).

body (17–1). Then drill axle peg holes, where indicated by the stars, through the front legs (17–3 and 17–4) and the back legs (17–5).

6. Cut a 1½″ length of ¼″ dowelling for the neck peg.

7. Apply glue to the neck peg and insert it into the neck hole in the head.

8. Glue the ears to the sides of the head (17–2) between the squares at the top.

9. Glue the nose to the head where indicated by the dashed oval on 17–2.

10. Split an 8-mm bead in half for the eyes. With the half-holes held vertically, glue the eyes to the head where indicated by the dots on 17–2.

11. Trim ¼″ from the ends of the axle pegs so that each measures 1″ from the top of the cap to the bottom of the peg.

12. Paint the body, head, legs, and axle peg caps

light grey-brown. (Don't paint the neck peg or into the neck and axle peg holes.)

13. Referring to 17–8, paint a thin light grey-brown ring around the eyes close to the head; paint the remaining parts of the eyes black. Use white to highlight each eye at 4 o'clock. Paint the nose dark brown, the chin beige, and the mouth medium pink. Use black to paint the mouth outline, chin detail, and tips of the front and back toes.

14. Apply the high-gloss finish to all parts.

15. To attach each leg, apply a small amount of glue into a peg hole in the body. Insert an axle peg through the peg hole in a corresponding leg and then into the glued peg hole in the body. The legs should be able to move up and down and hold a pose.

16. Using 17–6 for the pattern, cut two pieces of fake fur. Use tacky glue to adhere the fur to the backs of the ears.

17. For the whiskers, cut two ¼″ × ¼″ squares of fake fur. Use tacky glue to adhere the fur to either side of the mouth where indicated by the groups of squares on 17–2.

18. For the tail, cut a ⅜″ × ⅝″ rectangle of fake fur. Use tacky glue to adhere the tail between the squares on the body (17–1).

19. For the neck fur, cut a ½″ × 3⅝″ rectangle of fake fur. Overlap the ends ⅛″ to form a ring and secure with tacky glue.

20. To attach the head, insert the neck peg into the fur ring and then into the neck hole in the top of the body (do not glue). The head should be able to move from right to left.

17–8. Koala's face.

18. Tropical Fish Aquarium

Home to millions of beautiful tropical fish, the Great Barrier Reef of Australia is the largest structure ever built by living creatures. This 80,000-square-mile (204,800 sq km) reef consists mainly of coral and stretches for more than 1,250 miles (2,000 km) along the northeast coast of the Australian continent.

MATERIALS

- 20″ length of ¼ × ¾ clear pine lattice
- 60″ length of ¼ × 5¼ clear pine lattice
- 8″ length of ½ × 5½ clear pine lattice

- Drill bit: ¹⁄₁₆″

- 53″ length of #16-gauge brass wire
- Fourteen #19 × ½″ wire brads

- Wire cutters
- 5-gallon fish tank
- 10 pounds of aquarium gravel

- Acrylic paints: black, white, dark grey, medium yellow, medium orange, medium purple, terra cotta, light yellow-green, medium olive-green, and a color to match the gravel
- Acrylic metallic paints: light blue, black, medium blue, white, medium pink, and dark purple

Key to the photograph: (1) blue fish, (2) zebra fish, (3) castle, (4) yellow fish, (5) orange fish, (6) octopus, (7) crab, (8) coral, (9) short seaweeds, and (10) tall seaweed.

Refer to the color photo for the colors of all project parts.

#1, Blue Fish*

1. Cut four blue fish (18–1) from ¼ × 5¼ lattice.

2. Cut one stand base (18–2) from ½ × 5½ lattice.

3. Using the ¹⁄₁₆″ bit, drill ¼″-deep wire-support holes into three fish where indicated by the arrow on 18–1. After painting, set the fish without the drilled hole aside, to be used behind the castle (18–5).

4. Using the ¹⁄₁₆″ bit, drill ¼″-deep wire-support holes into the stand base (18–2) where indicated by the stars.

5. Paint the bodies light blue metallic. Use black to paint the gills and the body outline next to each fin. Paint the spots medium-blue metallic.

6. Paint the eyes white and the pupils black metallic.

7. Paint the stand base to match the gravel.

8. Refer to Table 1 to match the letter on the stand base (18–2) to the wire length needed; cut 3 pieces of wire of the lengths indicated in Table 1.

Table 1. Wires for Blue Fish

Stand-base letter	Wire length
A	2¼″
B	3⅝″
C	5¼″

9. To assemble, apply tacky glue to both ends of a wire and insert one end into the hole in the bottom of a fish and the other end into the corresponding hole in the stand base. Repeat for the other fish. Position the fish so that they face towards the left.

#2, Zebra Fish

1. Cut three zebra fish (18–3) from ¼ × 5¼ lattice.

2. Cut one stand base (18–4) from ½ × 5½ lattice.

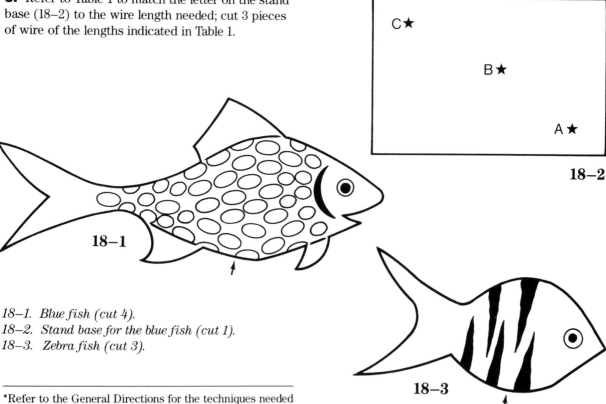

18–1. Blue fish (cut 4).
18–2. Stand base for the blue fish (cut 1).
18–3. Zebra fish (cut 3).

---

*Refer to the General Directions for the techniques needed to complete this project.

3. Using the ¹⁄₁₆″ bit, drill ¼″-deep wire-support holes into the fish where indicated by the arrow on 18–3.

4. Repeat Step 4 of the blue fish instructions.

5. Paint the bodies white metallic and the stripes black metallic.

6. Paint the eyes light blue metallic and the pupils black metallic.

7. Repeat Step 7 of the blue fish instructions.

8. Refer to Table 2 to match the letter on the stand base (18–4) to the wire length needed; cut 3 pieces of wire of the lengths indicated.

Table 2. Wires for Zebra Fish

Stand-base letter	Wire length
A	6″
B	7¾″
C	6¼″

9. Repeat Step 9 of the blue fish instructions, positioning the fish so that they face towards the right.

#3, Castle

1. Cut one castle (18–5) from ¼ × 5¼ lattice.

2. Cut a 6″ length of ¼ × ¾ lattice for the base.

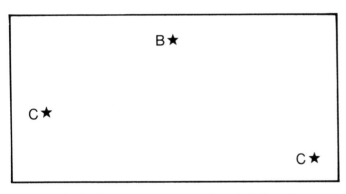

18–4

18–4. Stand base for the zebra fish (cut 1).
18–5. Half-pattern for the castle (cut 1).

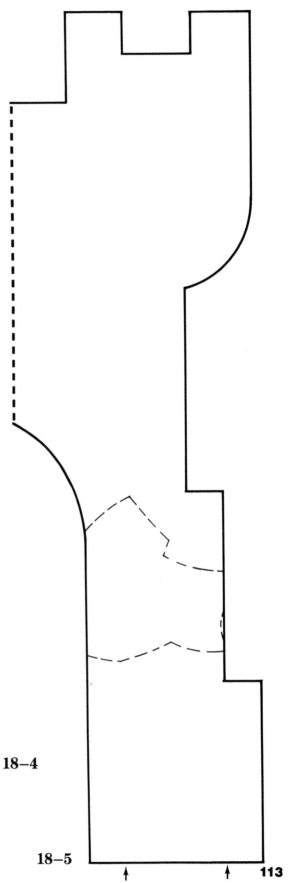

18–5

3. Apply glue to the bottom of the castle, and center it over the base. Nail brads through the base and into the castle where indicated by the arrows on 18–5.

4. Paint the castle dark grey and paint the base to match the gravel.

5. Use tacky glue to adhere the remaining blue fish (18–1) behind the right side of the castle, where indicated by the thin dashed lines in 18–5. Secure it with two brads nailed through the fish and into the castle.

General Directions for #4, Yellow Fish; #5, Orange Fish; and #6, Octopus

1. Using the appropriate pattern, cut the body from ¼ × 5¼ lattice.

2. For each, cut one 1¾″ × 2½″ stand base from ½ × 5½ lattice.

3. Using the ¹⁄₁₆″ bit, drill a ¼″-deep wire-support hole, where indicated by the arrow in the pattern.

4. Mark the center of the face of each stand base.

Using the ¹⁄₁₆″ bit, drill a ¼″-deep hole for the wire support.

5. Follow the painting directions given for each, and refer to the color photograph as needed.

6. Paint the stand bases to match the gravel.

7. Refer to Table 3 and match the fish or octopus to the wire length needed; cut 4 pieces of wire, as indicated.

Table 3. Wire Lengths for Yellow Fish, Orange Fish, and Octopus

Pattern	Wire length
Yellow fish	5¾″
Orange fish	4½″ and 5½″
Octopus	5½″

8. To assemble each, apply tacky glue to both ends of a wire and insert one end into the hole in the bottom of the fish or octopus and the other end into the hole in the stand base.

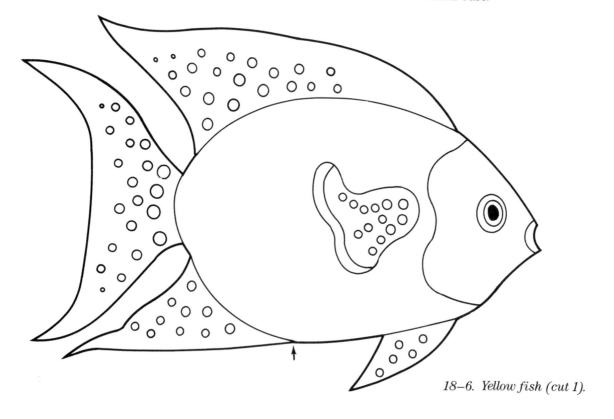

18–6. Yellow fish (cut 1).

#4, Yellow Fish

1. Cut one yellow fish (18–6) and one stand base.

2. Paint the body medium yellow and the fins black. Paint the face, the spots on the fins, and the edge of the side fins medium-pink metallic.

3. Use white to paint the eyes and mouth. Paint the pupils, eye outlines, and the center of the mouth black.

#5, Orange Fish

1. Cut two orange fish (18–7) and two stand bases.

2. Paint the bodies medium orange and the fins medium yellow.

3. Use white to paint the eyes and the outer border of the mouth. Paint the pupils black metallic.

4. Paint the gills and the front edge of the mouth black.

5. Using medium-blue metallic, paint the fin and tail outlines, the spots, the inner border of the mouth, and the eye irises.

#6, Octopus

1. Cut one octopus (18–8) and one stand base.

2. Paint the body medium purple and the spots dark purple metallic.

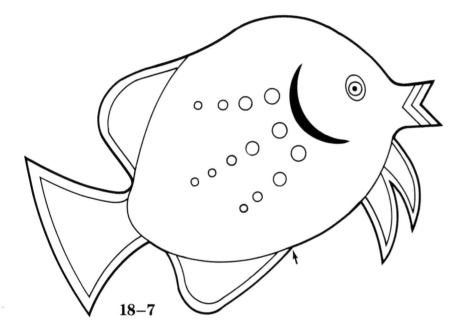

18–7

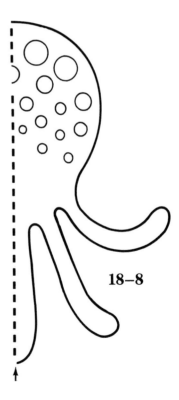

18–8

18–7. Orange fish (cut 2).
18–8. Half-pattern for the octopus (cut 1).

#7, Crab

1. Cut one crab (18–9) from ¼ × 5¼ lattice.

2. Paint the body medium-pink metallic, the eyes white metallic, and the pupils black.

#8, Coral; #9, Short Seaweeds; and #10, Tall Seaweed

1. Cut one coral (18–10), two short seaweeds (18–11), and one tall seaweed (18–12) from ¼ × 5¼ lattice.

2. For the bases, cut four 2¾″ lengths of ¼ × ¾ lattice.

3. To assemble each, apply glue to the bottom of a cutout and center it over a base. Nail brads through the base and into the cutout where indicated by the arrows on the appropriate pattern.

4. Paint the coral terra cotta; paint one short seaweed light yellow-green, the other medium olive-green, and the tall seaweed light yellow-green. Paint the bases to match the gravel.

Assembling the Tank

Pour the gravel into the tank. Bury the bases in the gravel. Lay the crab on the gravel. See the photograph for a suggested arrangement.

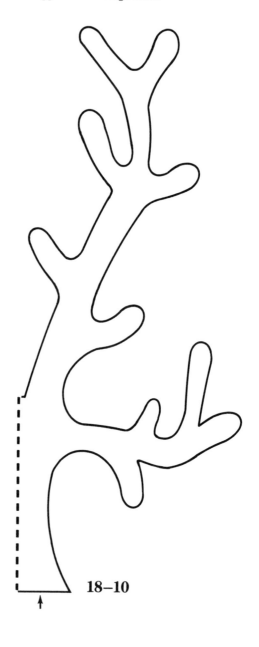

18–9. Half-pattern for the crab (cut 1).
18–10. Half-pattern for the coral (cut 1).

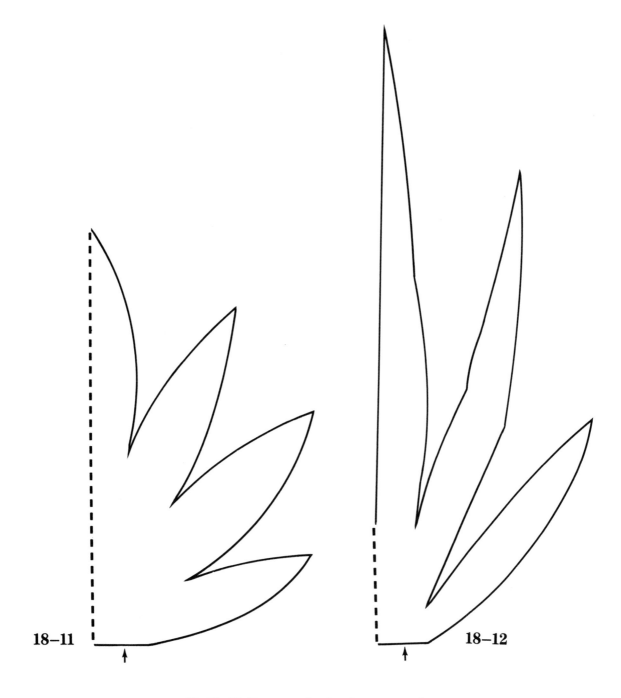

18–11

18–12

18–11. Half-pattern for the short seaweed
(cut 2).
18–12. Half-pattern for the tall seaweed
(cut 1).

19. Shark School Paddle Toy

Sharks have been around for more than 350 million years, and some species have remained unchanged for more than half that time. Their range is the tropical to temperate waters of the world, as far north as the Arctic Sea. There are 225 to 250 species and, of those, only 12 are menaces (such as the great white of Jaws fame). Sharks have a keen sense of smell and an endless supply of teeth. The tiger shark will produce, use, and shed 24,000 teeth over a 10-year period! Sharks range in size from 1 to 60 feet. Fortunately, the largest ones are the docile basking and whale sharks, which feed exclusively on plankton and shrimp.

MATERIALS

- 3″ length of ¼ × 5¼ clear pine lattice
- 20″ length of ½ × 5½ clear pine lattice
- Two 1¼″-long × ¼″-diameter wooden axle pegs
- Drill bits: ¹⁄₁₆″ and ⁷⁄₃₂″
- Six #4 × ¾″ flat-head wood screws
- Waterproof wood glue
- One 2¼″-long blue rubber band
- Acrylic paints: pale blue-grey, white, black, medium pink, and medium ultramarine
- Acrylic metallic paint: dark grey
- High-gloss waterproof finish

Shark School Paddle Toy*

1. Cut one small shark (19–1), one medium shark (19–2), one large shark (19–3), and one platform (19–4) from ½ × 5½ lattice.

2. Cut two paddles (19–5) from ¼ × 5¼ lattice.

---

*Refer to the General Directions for the techniques needed to complete this project.

3. Using the ¹⁄₁₆″ bit, drill ¼″-deep pilot holes into the lower edge of each shark where indicated by the arrows on the patterns.

4. Using the ¹⁄₁₆″ bit, drill pilot holes through the platform where indicated by the circles. The labels S, M, and L on the pattern indicates the corresponding size of shark (small, medium, or large) to be secured through the pilot holes.

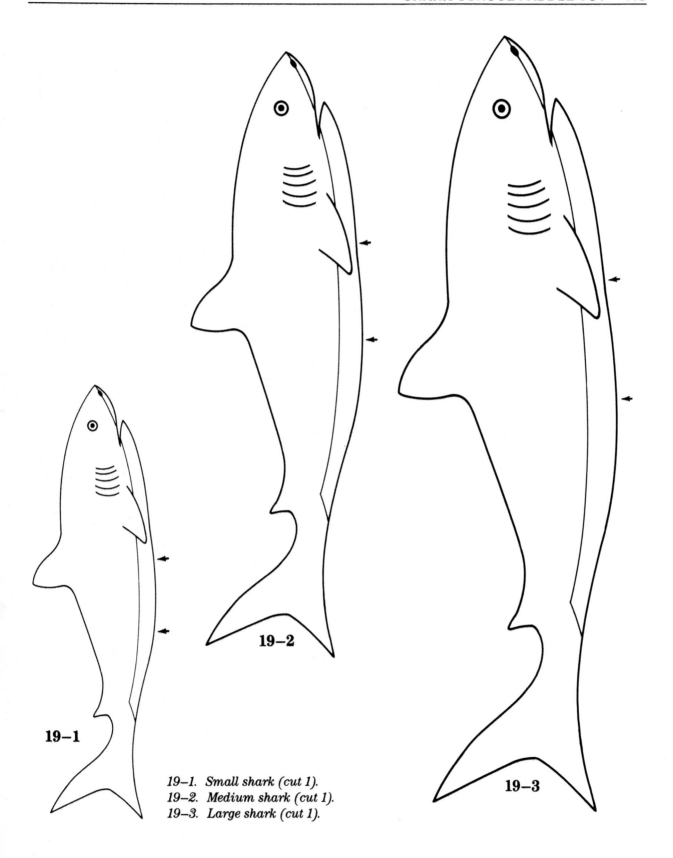

19–1. *Small shark (cut 1).*
19–2. *Medium shark (cut 1).*
19–3. *Large shark (cut 1).*

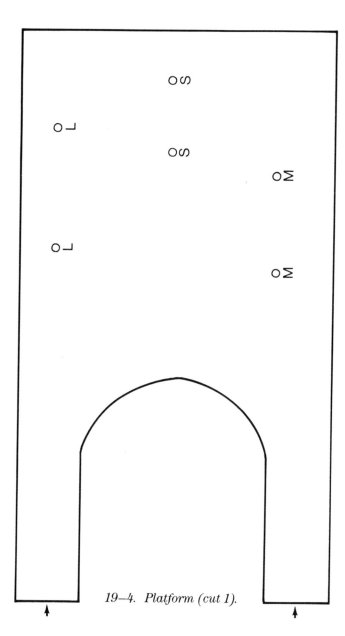

19–4. *Platform (cut 1).*

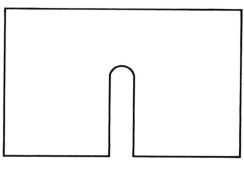

19–5. Paddle (cut 2).

5. Using the ⁷⁄₃₂″ bit, drill ¾″-deep peg holes into the center back of each platform arm where indicated by the arrows on 19–4.

6. Glue the axle pegs into the holes in the platform arms. To assemble the paddles, apply a small amount of glue to the inside edge of each paddle slot and slip one slot into the other.

7. Paint the sharks' upper bodies and fins dark grey metallic. Use pale blue-grey to paint the lower bodies, leaving the lower body edge between the pilot holes unpainted.

8. Paint the eyes white. Use black to paint the pupils, gills, and nostrils. Outline the side fins with black, as shown in the photograph.

9. Paint the mouth openings medium pink. For the teeth, make small drops of white paint, evenly spaced, along the inside edge of each upper mouth.

10. Apply glue to the bottom edge of each shark. Match the pilot holes in each shark to their corresponding pilot holes in the platform. Secure with screws inserted from the underside of the platform.

11. Paint the platform and paddle assembly medium ultramarine.

12. Apply the high-gloss waterproof finish to all parts.

13. Slip the rubber band around the paddles and then slip its ends over the pegs.

20. Pink Cockatoo

MATERIALS

- 50″ length of ¼ × 5¼ clear pine lattice
- 2″ length of ½ × 3½ clear pine lattice
- 10″ length of 1 × 10 clear pine
- 10″ length of ⅜″ dowelling
- 6″ length of ⅝″ dowelling

- One white 10-mm regular-hole round wood bead

- Drill bits: ¼″ and ⅜″

- One 1½″ red feather fluff
- 2″ × 2″ cellulose sponge

- Acrylic paints: very light grey (VLG), light grey (LG), light rose-pink (LRP), dark grey (DG), black (B), white (W), bright red (BR), dark red-brown, medium moss-green, and very dark grey-green
- High-gloss finish

A magnificent fan-shaped crest and lovely pink color make this Australian native, also called Major Mitchell's cockatoo, one of the prettiest of all the talking birds. The pink cockatoo is a forest dweller and feeds on plant seeds, plus roots and tubers, which it digs up with its bill. Pairs mate for life and will return to the same nesting hole for years.

Pink Cockatoo*

1. Cut one body (20–1) from 1 × 10 pine.

2. Cut one beak (20–2) from ½ × 3½ lattice.

3. Cut two back crests (20–3), one front crest (20–4), two legs (20–5), and two wings (20–6) from ¼ × 5¼ lattice. The leg pattern and the wing pattern show the orientation of the left leg and wing; the right leg and wing are mirror images.

4. Cut one each of the top, middle, and bottom tail feathers (20–7) from ¼ × 5¼ lattice.

5. Cut two ³⁄₁₆″ lengths of ⅝″ dowelling for the eye rings. Glue the eye rings to the sides of the head where indicated by the dashed circles on 20–1.

6. Split the 10-mm bead in half for the eyes. With the half-holes held horizontally, glue the eyes to the center of the eye rings. Fill the half-holes with paste wood filler, allow it to dry, and sand it smooth.

---

*Refer to the General Directions for the techniques needed to complete this project.

7. Glue the beak (20–2) to the front of the head between the arrows on 20–1.

8. Glue the first back crest (20–3) to the top of the head with its tip at the solid square on 20–1. Glue the second back crest (20–3) on top of the first with its tip at the open square on 20–1. Glue the front crest (20–4) to the second back crest, butting its tip to the second back crest's tip (see photo).

9. Glue the legs (20–5) to the sides of the body where indicated by the oval dashed line on 20–1.

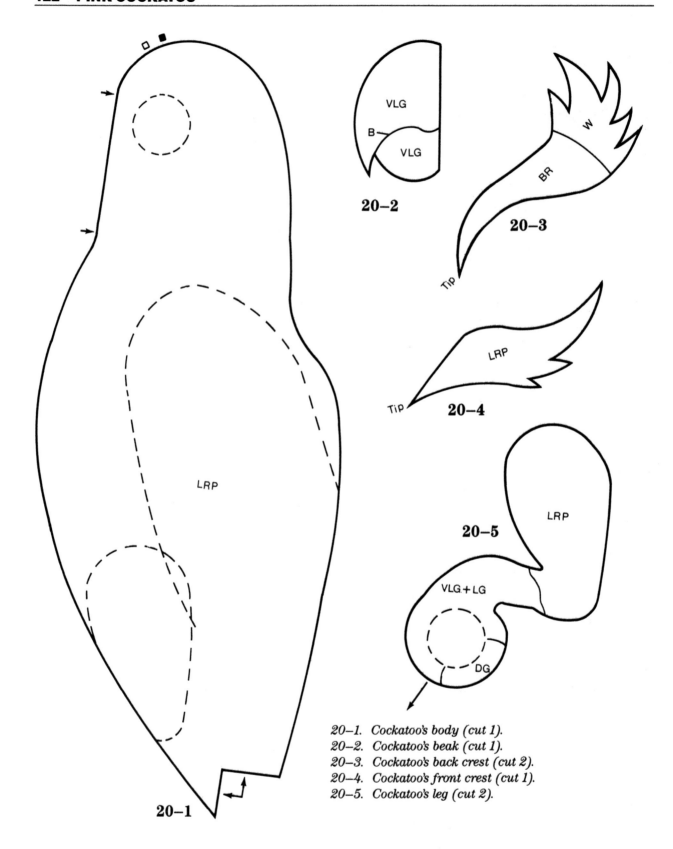

20–1. Cockatoo's body (cut 1).
20–2. Cockatoo's beak (cut 1).
20–3. Cockatoo's back crest (cut 2).
20–4. Cockatoo's front crest (cut 1).
20–5. Cockatoo's leg (cut 2).

10. To create the angle on the inside of each wing (20–6), whittle a flat surface from the dashed line to the star so that the thickness at the star is ⅛″.

11. Glue the wing angles to the body where indicated by the large curved dashed lines on 20–1. Glue the wings to the legs where they overlap.

12. Glue the top, middle, and bottom tail feathers (20–7) together. Have the straight ends aligned and centered on each other.

13. Glue the tail-feather assembly to the notch at the back of the body where indicated by the arrows on 20–1 (see photo).

14. Cut a length of ⅝″ dowelling; it should fit snugly between the feet without bowing out the legs. (This is the middle perch segment.) Cut two 1¼″ lengths of ⅝″ dowelling for the outer perch segments.

15. Using the ¼″ bit, drill a ⅜″ hole for the perch support into center of the length of the middle perch segment.

16. Glue the middle perch segment between the feet where indicated by the dashed circles on 20–5. Have the perch-support hole face in the direction of the arrow on 20–5.

17. Glue the outer perch segments to the outside of the feet where indicated by the dashed lines on 20–5.

18. Paint the lower legs and feet very light grey. Moisten the sponge with water and squeeze it almost dry. Dab the sponge into the light grey and tamp onto paper towelling to remove the excess. Dab over the lower legs and feet, making an irregular pattern. Referring to the Materials list for the colors, paint the rest of the cockatoo, as shown on 20–1 through 20–7 and on the color photograph. Extend the colors onto the edge surfaces.

19. Paint the eye rings white, the eyes dark red-brown, and the pupils black. Use black to paint the line between the upper and lower beak.

20. Paint the perch medium moss-green.

21. Apply the high-gloss finish.

22. Use tacky glue to adhere the feather fluff to the top of the head, as shown in the color photograph.

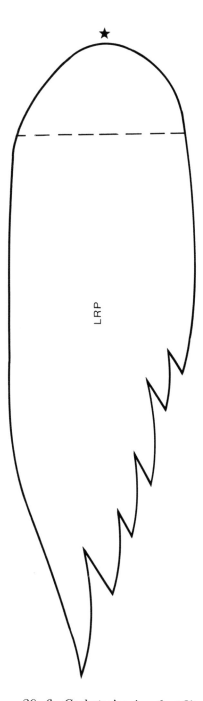

20–6. Cockatoo's wing (cut 2).

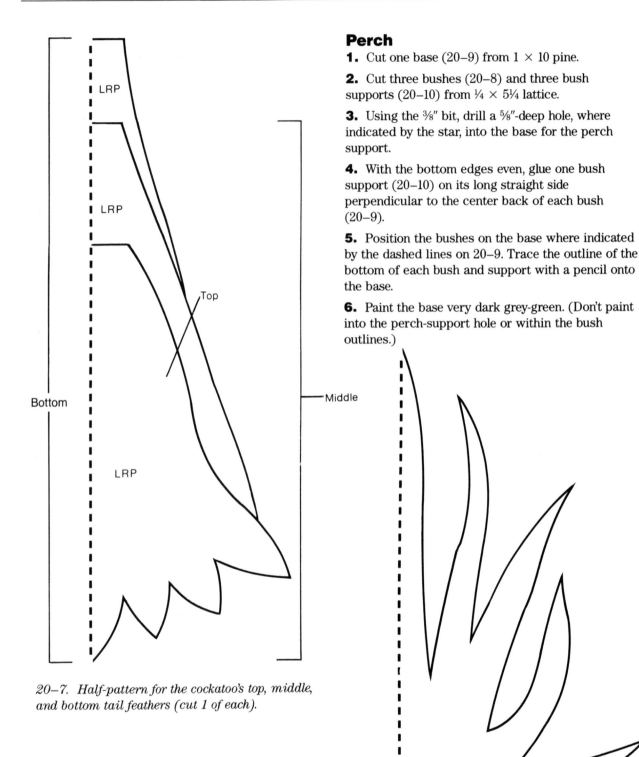

Perch

1. Cut one base (20–9) from 1 × 10 pine.

2. Cut three bushes (20–8) and three bush supports (20–10) from ¼ × 5¼ lattice.

3. Using the ⅜″ bit, drill a ⅝″-deep hole, where indicated by the star, into the base for the perch support.

4. With the bottom edges even, glue one bush support (20–10) on its long straight side perpendicular to the center back of each bush (20–9).

5. Position the bushes on the base where indicated by the dashed lines on 20–9. Trace the outline of the bottom of each bush and support with a pencil onto the base.

6. Paint the base very dark grey-green. (Don't paint into the perch-support hole or within the bush outlines.)

20–7. Half-pattern for the cockatoo's top, middle, and bottom tail feathers (cut 1 of each).

20–8. Half-pattern for the bush (cut 3).

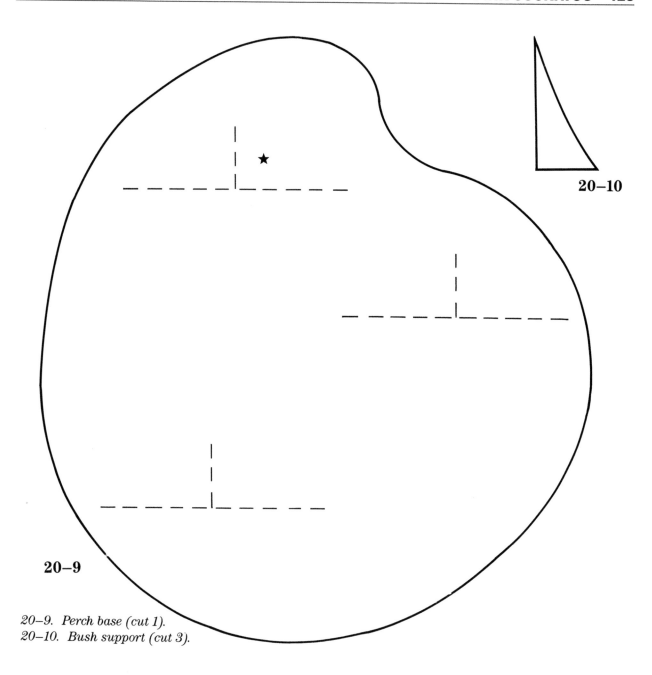

20–10

20–9

20–9. Perch base (cut 1).
20–10. Bush support (cut 3).

7. Paint the bushes medium moss-green. (Don't paint the underside of the bushes.) Glue the bushes to the base.

8. Use the 10″ length of ⅜″ dowelling for the perch support. Whittle ⅜″ of one end (top of the support) to a ¼″-diameter peg that fits snugly into the hole in the perch segment between the cockatoo's feet.

9. Paint the perch support medium moss-green.

(Don't paint the peg or ⅝″ of the bottom.)

10. Glue the unpainted bottom of the perch support into the hole in the base.

11. Apply the high-gloss finish to the base, bushes, and perch support.

12. To assemble, insert the peg end of the perch support into the hole in the middle perch segment between the cockatoo's feet.

Index

•••••••••••••

American Alligator, 35–38
Angles, whittling, 10
Asian Elephant Pull Toy, 98–106
Beads, cutting, 12
Bonding wood, 9, 11
Brushes, 8
Bullfrog, 17–20
Clamping, 8, 11, 12
Countersinking screws and brads, 12
Cutting wood, 9–10
Dowelling, how to cut, 10
Drilling holes, 11
Finishing, 13
General directions, 9–13
Giraffe Pull Toy, 70–77
Gluing, 8, 9, 10, 11–12
Goldfish Bowl, 82–88
Greater Pandas, 89–93
Holes, how to drill, 11
Koalas, 107–110
Left and right, 9
Lion Pull Toy, 64–69
Lumber sizes, 7
Materials, 7

Metric equivalents table, 127
Nail set, 8, 11
Paint, 7, 13
Patterns, 9
Pink Cockatoo, 121–125
Pond Slider Turtles, 39–41
Rattlesnakes, 21–25
Safety precautions, 8
Sanding, 8, 11
Scarlet Macaw, 42–50
Shark School Paddle Toy, 118–120
Spider Monkeys, 58–63
Stacking wood, 9
Tacky glue, 8, 12
Tiger Hobbyhorse, 94–97
Tools and equipment, 7–8
Toucan, 51–57
Transferring patterns and marks, 9
Tropical Fish Aquarium, 111–117
Whale and Dolphin Mobile, 30–34
Whittling, 10
Wood glue, 8, 12
Wood Duck Paddle Toys, 26–29
Zebra Hobbyhorse, 78–81

Metric Equivalents

• • • • • • • • • • • • •

INCHES TO MILLIMETRES AND CENTIMETRES

MM—millimetres   *CM—centimetres*

Inches	MM	CM	Inches	CM	Inches	CM
⅛	3	0.3	9	22.9	30	76.2
¼	6	0.6	10	25.4	31	78.7
⅜	10	1.0	11	27.9	32	81.3
½	13	1.3	12	30.5	33	83.8
⅝	16	1.6	13	33.0	34	86.4
¾	19	1.9	14	35.6	35	88.9
⅞	22	2.2	15	38.1	36	91.4
1	25	2.5	16	40.6	37	94.0
1¼	32	3.2	17	43.2	38	96.5
1½	38	3.8	18	45.7	39	99.1
1¾	44	4.4	19	48.3	40	101.6
2	51	5.1	20	50.8	41	104.1
2½	64	6.4	21	53.3	42	106.7
3	76	7.6	22	55.9	43	109.2
3½	89	8.9	23	58.4	44	111.8
4	102	10.2	24	61.0	45	114.3
4½	114	11.4	25	63.5	46	116.8
5	127	12.7	26	66.0	47	119.4
6	152	15.2	27	68.6	48	121.9
7	178	17.8	28	71.1	49	124.5
8	203	20.3	29	73.7	50	127.0